The Wisdom of Athor
Book One and Book Two

Messages from a Member of the Council of Twelve on the Etheric Plane of the Star System of Sirius

The Wisdom of Athor
Book One

Evelyn Fuqua Ph.D.

O.M.R.A. – Bandon, Oregon
2013

The Wisdom of Athor
Book One and Book Two

Messages from a Member of the Council of Twelve on the Etheric Plane of the Star System of Sirius

For information address:
P.O. Box 341
Bandon, Oregon 97411

www.evelynfuqua.com

Copyright © 2013
Printed and bound in the United States of America
Cover Design by Michael Phelan
First Printing 2013

ISBN   978-0-9850091-2-0

Published by
O.M.R.A.
Bandon, Oregon

"There are 16 dimensions interpenetrating this plane and this planet."

Aki/Athor

"Life is an evolving experiential process"
Aki/Athor

Dedicated to Aki, the indomitable woman who hosted the Athor spirit for 52 years

Table of Contents - Book One

About the Author

Evelyn Fuqua holds a B.A. in Psychology from Agnes Scott College, an M.A. in counseling from California State University Sacramento and a Ph.D. in Psychology from the Professional School of Psychology. She was a teacher, resource specialist and counselor in the public schools for 33 years. Dr. Fuqua served on the Board of Directors of the Association of Past Life Research and Therapy (presently International Association for Research and Therapies). She was State Relations Chairman for the California State Counselors Association. Fuqua has presented numerous workshops at professional conferences.

After retiring from the school system, she was in private practice as a Marriage, Family Therapist specializing in past life regression therapy and working with clients who are "Walk-Ins" or who have had other ET experiences.

Dr. Fuqua is the author of *From Sirius to Earth: A Therapist Discovers a Soul Exchange* and *Cosmic Relationships: Exploring the Soul's Journey from Off-Earth, Earth Lives, and Reincarnation.*

Evelyn is currently enjoying retirement on the Oregon coast with her mate Paul.

i

About Athor

There exists upon or within Sirius something akin to the so-called Garden of Eden. There is a Council of Elders, a group of beings who gather to determine what should be created and when. Then the determination is made as to where. There are twelve members of this council. They are Kyata, Phadrona (not exact but closest to Earth sound), Athor, Elysia, Philomyne, Achtama, Bjirdia, Gehema, Arturius, Sarta, Eloha and Badra.

The Council of Elders do not have physical bodies per se, but are merely a picture representation given to the mind to allow some type of visual recognition of frequencies. The Athor being has almost a warrior-type appearance. The visual impression brings forth a sash across the chest which is embedded with a logo similar to the lightning bolt coming through what appears to be a cloud. The eyes appear to be what you would term violet, sparkling violet eyes that give forth flashes of light. The nose is chiseled in what you term a Grecian form. The facial features are akin to those of Grecian nobility upon this plane and what is depicted as the Grecian gods.

The being Athor wears a kind of muted gray body suit which is like a second skin. There are boot-type looking things that appear to be of some other material, and they are a silver gray color. On these so-call boots, again the emblem of the lightning bolt appears. The hands are long, not unduly slender. The fingers are sensitive but very strong, and these are also covered in a long, glove-like thing which comes forth from the shoulder all the way to the fingers, covering all. It is almost like a uniform.

There is a collar of some sort that comes out and stands up, and the hair appears to be a very dark coloration of a most soft, extremely wavy texture, which is shoulder length. The being is seven and one-half to eight and one-half feet tall. Athor is androgynous, although the being has a very strong masculine energy.

The Sirian Council of Twelve is part of the Great White Brotherhood. There are twelve Councils that govern this universe; there are twelve members on each Council.

This book is in a question/answer format since that is the way I was able to obtain information from Athor. She would always say, "Ask me a question."

When asked how she is able to tap into the Akashic records, she replied, "There is a plane which exists between the fifth and sixth sublevels of the higher astral realms wherein are based what you term the Akashic records. It is herein that we turn to view that which you seek to know. It is herein that the bulk of what you term the soul's records of those who exist upon this plane are kept stored."

You use the name to tap into these records. How does that work?

"The name has an etheric frequency link with the individual who is presently embodied or disembodied as the case may be. It is through this link that these records are read."

Suppose a person marries and therefore, their present name changes with the new last name. How does that then affect the reading of these records?

"The name which is frequently used is that which carries the greatest link to that Being."

With all the billions of names on Earth, there must often be more than one individual with a particular name. How does that work in getting in touch with the soul vibration if there are one or more other people with the same name?

"Anytime that an individual has made a request through this channel or through your office as such for a reading, a link is made which is followed."

Athor frequently asked me to repeat a name during a reading. It was like she was seeing a motion picture and to get to the next frame she again needed the name. I do not use real names in these Athor Wisdom books since the material is highly confidential, but, of course, during the actual readings the real names were used. To avoid repetition I have usually eliminated the part where I am asked to repeat the name.

The material in Book One is mainly in response to my specific questions. Book Two is entirely soul readings in which Athor reads the soul's Akashic records.

Believe only what feels right to you. I only ask that you read these books with an open mind.

Preface

In late 1988 a client whom I called Rose (not her real name) came to me seeking assistance with her life-threatening condition of environmental illness. In the process of the therapy a Being named Athor surfaced. It was finally discovered that this Being entered the Rose physical vehicle when she was three years, two months old. The very involved story of why Athor entered such a damaged body required three years of therapy. The entire story is chronicled in my first book, *From Sirius to Earth*. Since that book was first published in 1997, I have learned that, in fact, Athor was probably not a true soul exchange as we had thought, but when Rose was a child the Athor being "overshadowed" the spirit of the child Rose. The energy of the Athor being was so intertwined with that of Rose that both she and I were convinced that she was indeed Athor, not Rose. However, in 2005 I learned that Athor had "walked out". This was upsetting news for all of us involved in the Athor case. It was after Athor left that Rose again was deep in her own analysis of her particular experiment and her conclusion about the overshadowing of the Rose spirit. In *Cosmic Relationships,* my second book, there is a chapter that goes into further detail about Athor leaving. I worked with Rose/Athor from 1988 through 2003 when she moved too far from my office for us to get together very often. We were first deeply involved in her therapy then in 1991 after realizing the fount of knowledge coming through Athor I began to ask my other clients if they would be interested in an Athor soul reading. She had an amazing gift of reading a person's Akashic records and connecting particular past lives with present day issues. The material used in Book One is from a newsletter that I published in 1996. While it contains material from some actual soul readings, it also gives answers to specific questions I asked Athor. Book Two of the Athor Wisdom is material taken from additional soul readings she did for many hundreds of clients who were generous enough to allow me to use their soul records for the good of greater humanity.

Chapter 1
The Great White Brotherhood

The Great White Brotherhood is comprised of an infinite number of Beings who are involved with galactic systems, star systems, planetary systems, etc. They are Beings who have remembered the oneness of the All That Is, and they are aware of that oneness, and yet they are simultaneously aware of the individualized differentiations coexisting within that oneness. Thus there are those of the White Brotherhood who are involved particularly with the planet Earth itself and have chosen to deal with individualized differentiations and the manners of consciousness on the surface of this planet you call Earth. These Beings who have chosen to deal with this planet have done so out of love, respect and gratitude for the All That Is for the manifestation of such a beauteous planetary sphere. There are those others of the Great White Brotherhood who are dealing with other systems as well. So to believe that the Ones that have been channeled for many years through the Bailey material and many other sources as well, that these are the only beings that comprise the so-called White Brotherhood is not correct for there is an infinite number of Beings and consciousnesses that can loosely be termed as part of the Great White Brotherhood. The term itself is rather unfortunate because it bespeaks of a certain racial quality which is not intended, so the terminology should be adjusted to indicate the Beings who have seen and know the All That Is. These Beings, whoever and wherever they may be, are indeed all those in the so-called White Brotherhood because once a Being remembers the fact that all is indeed one then that Being can only function from that oneness, neither discriminates nor allows for any types of divisions or separations within its

1

consciousness. For all is contained within its consciousness. There will be many who will continue to use the term Great White Brotherhood, and that is okay for those who do not misunderstand the term. Again perhaps those who become aware of the so-called racial aspects of this name would begin to look for a better terminology.

Chapter 2
Athor's Connection with the Egyptian Goddess Hathor

Athor: The Athor Being is an energy conglomerate of much greater proportions than what is coming through this vehicle at this time. The Athor energy has put down an aspect of itself through this Being, this body of the Rose Being. The Hathor Being was another such aspect, thus the memory is intimately and intricately involved in the higher levels of the representations of the Athor Being, and in particular each ray that is brought forth from that consciousness.

Dr. Fuqua: How did Hathor arrive here on Earth?

Athor: This was a simple matter of transcending time and space, and appearing at will in whatever location desired.

Dr. Fuqua: So it was not an actual spaceship vehicle in which Hathor came to Earth?

Athor: No. The Being spent what you would term a great deal of time in this mode of traveling, so to speak, back and forth. It did not remain on this planet as a resident, but it made many sojourns, many trips, wherein it came to give of itself to share and to maintain a certain level of what had begun here on the planet.

Dr. Fuqua: In Earth time, when did Hathor first come to Earth?

Athor: The Hathor form energy representation came approximately three million years ago.

Dr. Fuqua: What place on Earth did Hathor first appear?

Athor: I'm getting a blank.

Dr. Fuqua: It supposedly was Egypt. (When I flew to Egypt in 1994 with a group of Rosicrucians the Egyptian Airline had a large mural of Hathor on the interior wall of the plane. I found that in Egypt many people used the names Athor and Hathor interchangeably. There is a large temple dedicated to Hathor.)

Athor: We don't know this; it precedes the Vedic texts of India.

Hathor first touched down in Mesopotamia.

Dr. Fuqua: That is the so-called Cradle of Civilization, the Tigris-Euphrates Valley region where humankind seemed to take a giant leap forward in its evolution. When Hathor would touch down here on Earth, would she become physicalized? Did she always retain the same physical appearance or did her shape shift?

Athor: No, her/its appearance changed.

Dr. Fuqua: Did Mesopotamia date back three million years?

Athor: This is not what you are imagining that there were hordes and hordes of Beings and that there were large so-called cities and things of that sort. That is not the case.

Dr. Fuqua: At that time, three million years ago, when Hathor first came to Earth, was there still a semblance of a Garden of Eden?

Athor: Not on the surface.

Dr. Fuqua: It had already gone inside the Earth?

Athor: Yes.

Chapter 3
Earth's Early Years

Dr. Fuqua: What kind of Beings did Hathor encounter on Earth three million years ago?

Athor: They were of a rudimentary and somewhat crude nature. As there had been many experimental 'stations' shall we say, set up on the surface of this planet, and many Beings were transported; they were 'cloned' elsewhere and transported and dropped off here, so to speak, in different parts of this planet. And so there was quite a hodgepodge. There was a hodgepodge of different types of Beings, most of them of a rather rudimentary nature. The hand structures were quite different from the present day human hand as it is seen that many of these Beings had approximately three digits instead of five, and the toes were similar. They did not have five toes. Some had less and some had more. The toes were of a splayed nature which was sort of a mix between amphibious and human. Some had webs between their toes, others still had scales or remnants of the reptilian nature. It is seen there were many different life forms on the face of this Earth. Many of them walked in an upright pose, but the frequencies and vibrations were not of an enlightened type of race or anything of that sort. It was just a melting pot at that time. It was seen that the Hathor Being, among others, was making continual trips between the Center of the planet and the surface bringing forth some of this energy, because it is seen that in a sense a great darkness had descended on the surface of the planet with these various experimental modes going on and this planet was a 'dumping ground'. It was similar to the English taking their prisoners to Australia in the past. This was very similar to what happened here.

5

Dr. Fuqua: In *The Sirius Mystery,* the author Robert Temple discusses the theory about the Dogan tribes in Africa whose legends tell of the earliest Beings here who were somewhat like amphibians.

Athor: They did not originate here. These were cloned genetically.

Dr. Fuqua: Did they come from a spaceship to the water and would they then actually come out of the water as according to legend?

Athor: Yes, many groups used many of the substances found on the planet itself to experiment with and try to create a different type of life form. It is seen there were at least between thirty and forty different groups that experimented and dumped their offspring here.

Dr. Fuqua: Do you mean they experimented somewhere else?

Athor: Yes.

Dr. Fuqua: And then they dumped their offspring on Earth?

Athor: They experimented with the substances taken from the planet and the Beings on the planet. You see there was such a hodgepodge of experimentation going on that it was basically, quite frankly, a free for all. This was not intended by the Beings who brought the formation of this planet into existence. However, that is what occurred, and so three to four million years ago there was a great darkness on the surface of the planet. There was a physical darkness somewhat similar to what you now only have in places near the Arctic Circle. This permeated the entire planetary sphere because there were many factors here wherein there were cosmic energies, cosmic dust particles, things of this sort. The Earth itself was in a different position to the Sun. There were asteroid belts and cosmic dust belts above the surface of the

6

planet. It had a different gaseous structure in the atmosphere. There were many things that were quite different from what you see today. So the Beings of that time were very rudimentary because how else could they survive in such types of atmosphere?

Dr. Fuqua: At that point in time, what was the animal population like? What did these beings eat? Were they animal hunters? Were there dinosaurs at that point?

Athor: The dinosaurs were in large part, almost like actual transplants from other systems. They were, in a sense, rudimentary life forms, but they were not so rudimentary like some of these humanoid looking shapes that were cloned and genetically produced and so forth; because it is seen that these reptilian forms and dinosaur forms actually came here from other systems, and they were almost left intact. They were not experimented with and upon as the humanoid forms were; in fact, the dinosaur consciousness was of a higher nature than the humanoid forms walking on the planet at that time. They had a craftiness and a cunning that indicated almost a higher level of intelligence. They were, however, extremely carnivorous, although not all of them. They did not think twice, so to speak, as any wild animal does not think twice in getting something to eat. Basically because of their size, because of their locomotion, because of the remnants of historical references which humans have today, human beings thought that the dinosaurs were of a very low evolutionary scale. That is not the case.

Dr. Fuqua: Where did the dinosaurs originate? What system?

Athor: I hear Andromeda. It is seen that the eggs and the seeds were brought, not the entire grown form as such. They were well cared for and not just simply dropped off here. You see, this system had a better ecological setup than where these Beings came from originally. For it is seen that where these cosmic dust belts were around the Earth, they were in a phase where they were starting to leave when the dinosaurs were on the face of the planet. The place that they came from, the environmental factors were such that they were not compatible with those life forms.

Dr. Fuqua: With all of this hodgepodge of humanity down here, how could Hathor really help with this? It sounds like a grand mess!

Athor: Indeed it was. It required a constant period of monitoring, which spanned in the Hathor essence thousands of years.

Dr. Fuqua: Well, does the monitoring mean that Hathor didn't interfere, just monitored to see what was going on?

Athor: Pretty much until a certain period of time.

Dr. Fuqua: Let's take it to the first step upward in some kind of evolutionary pattern, getting out of that time period of a really terrible mess.

Athor: There were gigantic and cataclysmic upheavals both on the surface of the planet as well as coming from within the planet itself. There were tremendous earthquakes, volcanic type eruptions and formations and just major upheavals, such as has never been witnessed, not even at the time of the Great Flood.

Dr. Fuqua: Give me an approximate time period when this was happening.

Athor: Two and a half million years ago.

Dr. Fuqua: So any evidence of any of those creatures that were here at that time in terms of humanity was pretty much destroyed. After that great cataclysmic event, then what happened?

Athor: It is seen that there was a resurgence and a rebirth which does not seem to be so physical. It appears to be more in a 'Devic' sense. I don't know how to interpret this. I'm seeing images that are very beautiful of plants and things of this sort. I didn't see them forming, but I see them now; it was lush vegetation. It is seen that this took approximately ten thousand years.

Dr. Fuqua: Were the dinosaurs all killed in that upheaval or did they manage to survive?

Athor: It is seen the civilization which brought them here in the first place had not died out, and the ones who remained, these were not ones who had the enormous bulk of the Earth-based dinosaurs. But they were of the reptilian nature, these Beings. They replanted some of these Beings. It was really quite due to the nature of the surface of this planet, the atmospheric conditions and various things that they had because they were not of that size elsewhere.

Dr. Fuqua: Were these dinosaurs relatives of the Reptilians?

Athor: Yes.

Dr. Fuqua: They were like a mutant type variety?

Athor: They simply replanted their species back on the surface when they saw conditions seemed to appear to be favorable as such.

Dr. Fuqua: Since these dinosaurs were so destructive in terms of eating people, etc. what was the motivation for replanting them here on Earth?

Athor: What is the purpose of having tigers and wolves, leopards and jaguars upon the surface of the planet? They all must exist as well.

Dr. Fuqua: How did the reptilians survive all these earthquakes and cataclysmic events?

Athor: As was stated, they survived because they were repopulated.

Dr. Fuqua: During these cataclysmic times did any human form, even rudimentary human forms, survive?

Athor: No.

Dr. Fuqua: So there was total destruction of the entire Earth?

Athor: Yes, and there was not enough interest by the Creator forces of these rudimentary forms to swoop down and save them because they basically saw what had resulted from their experiments and they were not pleased with it themselves.

Dr. Fuqua: So it was an experiment gone bad, and they just did away with it.

Athor: Yes.

Dr. Fuqua: Okay, let's go to the next major step in evolution. When did mankind first start being repopulated down here?

Athor: Approximately one and a half to two million years ago.

Dr. Fuqua: What took place?

Athor: Some of these initial Beings who had been responsible for these horrendous mutant forms, learned considerably from their first experiment. And they set about to do a better job, so to speak. And it is seen that other groups came in and some of the old groups that had been members dropped out of this whole experiment. So it was infused with what might be called 'new blood' here. They began to experiment and form different species of humanoid type creatures that were similar to their own types or what they wished to create. They had a much better understanding of what they did not wish. In the very beginning, anything went regarding experimentation, and that is why there was such a horrific mess and a hodgepodge of creatures here. Some had one eye, some had three, some had this and some that, and each creature was a life form almost unto itself. They could be cloned, but basically what was the use? They saw nothing productive in cloning any of these particular species they had originally created on the Earth, and so from that first experiment they realized what they did not want. Of course they did not see the sum totality because some of the Beings who were involved in the population of this planet did not then have the capacity to see all the possible twists and turns of what these life forms might evolve into on their own. It was seen some of the Beings did not wish to stand guard and be there all the time to make sure that the Beings went in a certain direction. This was all an experimental phase and they just simply had learned what they did not want. But they did not have the ability to look ahead far enough to see what might happen and how to stave off what might happen because there were other factors that came into effect because of the cosmic cycles of that particular phase. The planet one and a half to two million years ago entered a phase wherein the cosmic currents were such that whatever was brought here had to be allowed to basically evolve on its own. This is not to say it did not receive assistance, but it changed the nature of everything. Because the Creator Gods no longer had the ability at that point to totally structure, guide, watch, etc. to just put a clamp on everything and make it turn out the way they wanted.

Dr. Fuqua: You are talking about the creator gods and not the Council of Sirius. Let me be clear. You are talking about different Creator gods from different systems.

Athor: Yes; different species from many systems.

Dr. Fuqua: When all of these different kinds of experiments started going on, did all the members of the Adamic race go to the center of the Earth?

Athor: Yes. They are not in physical existence. The Beings who claim to be from under Mount Shasta are a different race and of a different order.

Dr. Fuqua: I see. Then the very center of the Earth is different.

Athor: Yes. Therein resides the Garden of Eden. The term Creator Gods is loosely used to describe those Beings who create other Beings whether it is in an etheric or a physical form. It is not to simply describe those who create souls. Those are also Creator Gods but of a different order.

Dr. Fuqua: The beings who were of the mutant type that were here on Earth millions of years ago, did they have 'souls" per se?

Athor: No. That is one reason there was such great chaos. There was no higher force, no higher energy and so also there was no karmic debt in their destruction.

(The session with Athor ended at this point. I have been asked many times what went wrong with the Earth experiment since the original matrix (blueprint) by the Council of Sirius was designed to be like a "Garden of Eden". The Biblical story of Adam and Eve and eating the fruit from the tree of knowledge of good and evil goes into the next phase of the Earth's history when man was given free will. This again led to many poor decisions by humankind which has brought us to this present state of chaos on Earth. At this point in time we are being given much assistance from the Beings of Light to prevent another huge cataclysmic event (nuclear war, etc.).

I want to repeat an invocation given to my mate Paul and myself by Athor back in 2011. Please join us in saying this on a daily basis. It is short and can be easily memorized.

"We are surrounded by a circle of White Light. We ask that all the Beings of Light who would like to assist in bringing peace, harmony, good will and balance to the Earth to do so. We invoke the highest beings of Light to protect the Earth and its inhabitants."

Chapter 4
Ascended Masters

Dr. Fuqua: What is your definition of an Ascended Master? (Athor does not particularly relate to the Ascended Masters since the Council of Twelve is a different evolutionary line, but many of my clients related very strongly to particular Masters, therefore, I wanted Athor's definition.)

Athor: An Ascended Master is a being who has completed the karmic cycles. It not only has completed the karmic cycles, but it has transmuted the essence of the physical atomic structure into that of pure Light and has thus ascended. There are no physical remnants of its former self which it last inhabited.

Dr. Fuqua: Where did they originate before they began their Earth cycles?

Athor: As a rule they are not considered Ascended Masters before completing the Earthly cycles. There are those of other dimensional frequencies which might be termed Ascended Masters depending on their particular evolutionary cycles, but the ones that this Being is referring to are the ones who have come through the Earth rounds, whether coming through the complete rounds or coming from elsewhere and then completing here.

Dr. Fuqua: They could come from almost anywhere in the universe. Is this true?

Athor: Yes. They come from all areas of the universe.

Chapter 5
Destruction of Planet Maldek

Dr. Fuqua: You did a reading for a woman who was on Maldek and the planet was destroyed. Can you give us more information about this?

Athor: The so-called semi-physical etheric structure of it was entirely annihilated. This particular energy source shredded and restructured all energies which it could consume. It could not, however, restructure the energies of the spiritual realm and spiritual frequencies such as the soul bodies and Light bodies of spiritual beings. It could consume and shred all matter that was of a denser nature than that of pure Light.

Dr. Fuqua: What was the reason for Maldek being destroyed?

Athor: It would appear that the beings upon this planet called Maldek had experiments with various type energies and permutations and the result of which an opening was made which allowed this particular energy pattern to come through. Up until that time this energy was in another dimensional frequency and in another configuration. With the experimentation in which the beings engaged on this system, the energy field opened up allowing this other life form to come through. There are many, many different energy forms in the universe and each system has a particular protective ring in the atmosphere which protects the system from certain frequencies which come through as, for instance, your Earth's ozone layer and other layers which allow the sun's rays to come forth in a certain spectrum. They do not allow the full force of the rays to come through because if that were the case, the life forms upon this planet would cease to exist. So it is the case of other systems as well. Depending upon their various levels of density, they have their various protective rings around their particular systems. This ring on Maldek was disturbed, and as a consequence, the entire life forms were annihilated.

Dr. Fuqua: What was the nature of the physical forms upon Maldek?

Athor: These beings did not have the humanoid features that the Earth beings have today. These beings were more of your space alien-looking type beings. They appeared to have antenna-like structures coming forth from the tops of the head, and they had a somewhat amphibious looking appearance, but the skin texture was of a somewhat leathery consistency, and it would appear to be a somewhat greenish color.

Dr. Fuqua: In terms of Earth time, about how long ago did planet Maldek exist?

Athor: It would appear to be about 580 billion years ago.

Dr. Fuqua: Was the Earth in existence at that time?

Athor: No.

Dr. Fuqua: Was Maldek in our Solar system?

Athor: No

Dr. Fuqua: Was it in another galaxy?

Athor: Yes.

Dr. Fuqua: How long was Maldek actually in existence?

Athor: One to two billion years. But you must understand that linear time frames are not accurate ones. You are asking for numbers in relation to your particular time frame reference. The time spectrum is quite different in other systems, and in fact, there is no time as such because indeed all time is simultaneous. Trying to relegate it to a static number is not really an accurate representation of the facts.

Dr. Fuqua: How many people here on Earth had had some kind of existence on Maldek?

Athor: About 2%.

Dr. Fuqua: About how many had had existences on Mars?

Athor: 4-5%.

Dr. Fuqua: About how many have had existences on Venus?

Athor: 7-8%.

Dr. Fuqua: What about Jupiter?

Athor: 2-3%

Dr. Fuqua: Uranus?

Athor: 1%

Dr. Fuqua: Mercury?

Athor: 7%

Dr. Fuqua: Pluto?

Athor: 4%

Dr. Fuqua: Neptune?

Athor: 7%

Dr. Fuqua: The moon?

Athor: Approximately 13%

Dr. Fuqua: Saturn?

Athor: 6%. Considering the entire world population these are rather high percentages. What you will find is that there are an increasing number of beings coming to the planet at this time and already here as well who have had existences on star systems as opposed to planetary systems. It would seem that these are becoming more in the majority at this time.

Dr. Fuqua: (I have conducted Athor readings for several clients who are severely depressed, and when asked to go to the root cause of their depression, Athor began going into an existence on Maldek during the period when the planet was destroyed. Apparently this trauma left a deep impression in the psyche of these souls. In these cases anti-depressants did not help their depression, but knowing the root cause of the depression seemed to improve their mental outlook to some degree. Book Two contains actual readings for clients who lived on Maldek.)

Chapter 6
The Photon Belt

Dr. Fuqua: What can you tell us about the photon belt? (Keep in mind that this information came through in 1996 when there was much talk in metaphysical circles about the photon belt. It would seem that much of this information ties into the energies coming to the Earth during the 2012 period and appear to be ongoing as Athor states.)

Athor: The term photon belt means nothing to us (meaning the Council). We are trying to tap into the energy of your terminology. (Long pause). It is seen there are certain cosmic rays which are in various configurations converging upon the planet Earth as the results of the entire cosmic changes. There are certain cosmic rays which are converging. Some of these rays are converging upon the face of the planet as a whole. They are basically coming forth simultaneously in all points of your Earth's atmospheric outer ring. The other cosmic rays are only impinging on certain specific sites of juncture points upon the planetary surface itself.

The so-called terminology of photon belt we find to be rather inadequate. The magnitude of the galactic rays is such that they far transcend anything dealing with any optical photon type of particle. These are not the exact representations of the particles which are bombarding the surface of your planet. The closest description that we can give again is cosmic rays. The energies of these cosmic rays are designed to accentuate the development of various species. The cosmic rays are not directed by any being nor are they directed by any group of beings. They are simply a by-product of the entire changes both within this solar system and beyond.

There is a tremendous energetic upheaval in major parts of your Milky Way. There are certain star systems which are presently also undergoing various bombardments of cosmic energies. The by-products of all of this are the cosmic rays which are basically bombarding the Earth at this time. What has already happened in certain star systems eons ago is only now in terms of the cosmic rays and energies coming toward the surface of this planetary sphere. This particular universe is a self-perpetuating entity which in a sense breathes. In the process of breathing there are certain by-products which occur as in the process of respiration. The energy of the creative force breathes, and in one breath of that creative force which sustains the entire universe there are tremendous by-products of changes that occur. Because the one breath of that creative force sustaining this universe contains everything within it - all the planets, all the stars, all the existences within it are affected in the process of that breath. That breath takes eons and eons of time for one breath, but nonetheless in the process of it there is great destruction, there is great creation, and there are many changes on levels that humans cannot even begin to comprehend.

So these energies which are coming here at this time are the by-products of this breath. They impact the Earth, but they are much, much greater than that, and the impact that they are having on the Earth is what these energies are in the process of doing. They are beginning to make the Earth breathe as a spirit, as a Being. The Earth as a Being needs these energies to survive as a planet. They are not so much designed for humans. This is a byproduct of the entire nature of the universal scheme, and those of you who would think that there are beams being specifically sent to Earth at this time, that is incorrect. They are being beamed in the balance of the universal scope as a byproduct of that great creative force. The impact on the Earth is that the Earth must breathe, and it will set about a chain reaction within the planetary sphere where the spirit of the Earth will begin to breathe. As this occurs, there will be more and greater cataclysmic changes on the surface of the planetary system which will indirectly affect human beings and all life forms upon the surface of the planet. It is possible that there will be some degree of darkness, but we do not see this as a given. We see more the results of the Earth's planetary reactions. The Earth as a planetary sphere is much more directly connected to these energies than each human vehicle. It is difficult to describe exactly how because human beings also resonate on this energy level. What these rays CAN do - first of all they are very powerful rays of energy, and they will align all energies in the path that they encompass. They will align all energies to a certain set of frequency ranges. Anything below that frequency range will not survive. That does not mean it will physically annihilate, but it will not survive on a frequency level of consciousness. The energies will align frequencies so that they will match the frequencies of the rays because the Earth is in a great upheaval. It must be stabilized.

The energies are more akin to the nature of the planetary system than they are to the various life forms upon it. The human kingdom has generated so many different types and odd forms of frequencies that there is a huge hodgepodge here. These cosmic rays would basically eliminate a lot of those frequencies. It is a certain harmonic which is coming to the surface of this planet. It is the end result of the creative breath of the force of this universe. This is really simply one of the by-products.

It is always wise to go within to the deepest source within your own soul, within your own heart, within your own psyche to see what resonates of what it is you read and hear. Sometimes it is difficult because what is read and heard seems to make sense to the logical processes of the human mind, and many times it makes sense to the part of the mind that seeks adventure, which seeks revelation, which seeks the exciting and the new, but there is a balance in all things, and sometimes it is difficult because of those parts of the mind getting more of a control to determine exactly what is the truth and what is not. So this is always an ongoing process which each individual must determine on an almost daily basis for them. That is basically what we would wish to add.

The attempt should always be for an individual to seek the highest and most truthful and clearest source of truth within and bring all data to that place and to also work on one's self so that place is cleaned frequently and expanded as one continues. So basically the nature of the energies from our viewpoint are not what they would seem from the human mind. But we do not minimize the fact that they are very powerful, and the changes which are to happen to try to translate what we have said to a smaller level to what it will do in each individual case is erroneous. There are so many factors involved. If you take an energy that aligns frequencies, then each vehicle would have a unique reaction to that. Some would indeed self-destruct. Others would not, so to label this thing as the Photon Belt and to say in such a limited fashion that people will do this and they will do that is not accurate. The scope of the energies is much, much beyond that. We presently do not see that there is a great likelihood of accurately giving a detailed interpretation of those energies.

Dr. Fuqua: Can you give a time period in which these energies will hit full force?

Athor: Within a period of your time line of 50 to 150 years there will be such a change upon this planet. These are not drastic changes in the sense that there will be an entirely different life form. It will be drastic in the sense of the level of consciousness which the beings will have. It will be drastic in the sense in which the manners of government and relating in a social fashion will have changed. There will be much more uniformity of thought patterns which you see presently because at present you have an enormous hodgepodge of different energies upon this plane; there will be a greater homogeneity, but that is not about to be for a period of approximately 50 years.

Chapter 7
Walk-Ins - Many Kinds of Experiments

Over the years when I was in private practice, a number of clients who had sudden profound changes in personality came to me for therapy. I usually sensed that the person was probably of the Walk-In category, but I could not determine just which experiment had taken place. Usually their therapy with me was fairly brief because what they really needed to know is what happened to them to cause the drastic change in personality. I would usually tell them about Athor and suggest an Athor reading. To date we have found the following classifications, although you should keep in mind that each experiment is indeed unique. (1) Soul Exchange (2) Future aspect of the person's own soul (3) Integration of the group soul (4) Soul Braids (5) Brain utilization expansion (6) Experimentation on the brain and physical body by extraterrestrials. (7) Overshadowing of a soul by an extraterrestrial as in the case of Athor. There are no doubt many other explanations, but thus far, these are the only type of cases I have documented through individual Athor readings.

A far more common phenomenon is the opening of the Higher Self into one's consciousness. While this transformation may not be as dramatic, it can create many problems in relationships, the work place, etc. since the person no longer seems to fit into mainstream thinking. This phenomenon can often be determined through hypnotherapy work without an Athor reading, and this kind of experience is one I encountered with my clients quite often.

People have often asked if Near Death experiences are the same as Walk-In experiments. While many Walk-Ins claim to have had Near Death experiences, I do not believe that everyone who has gone through a Near Death experience is a

Walk-In because they do not have the feeling that they are a different person, although they often have a very different spiritual outlook on life.

Chapter 8
Soul Braids

I have had three cases of the Soul Braid type of Walk-In experiment. While this is a general classification, each case seems unique to the particular soul choices of that individual.

In 1992 a young man, age 20, came to see me for therapy. David (not real name) stated that he really didn't know why he had come except his mother had been one of my clients and she thought I might be able to help her son whom she felt is quite unusual. After taking a case history I was really puzzled by David who seemed to have far more wisdom than any 20 year old I had ever known before. He had read many philosophical books although he had dropped out of high school due to difficulties in coping with "the system". David had no career goals. He worked in the family business part time and spent much of his other time babysitting his ten brothers and sisters. He did this with apparently no resentment. Although he is an extremely good looking young man, he had never had a girlfriend.

During the second session we began the hypnotic process, but it was seemingly impossible for him to go into a trance state. I, therefore, suggested an Athor reading to which he readily agreed.

Athor first identified a probe in David's auric field which was attached in a life cycle many, many years ago. In that cycle David was a Being with a grayish, bluish color skin which was shiny and smooth, with large eyes. He seemed to be visiting Earth conducting research. The Being was from a very technological civilization, and the probe had to do with transmitting data. Athor determined that this incarnation was David's first experience in a human body on Planet Earth which explains why David is so different from the usual man his age and has difficulty coping with everyday life.

In further examining the auric field, Athor stated, "The entire arrangement of this energy field has more loose spaces within it in order for it to allow different energies and frequencies to come into it. This is very different from possession. It is an energy body designed to accommodate another energy that will merge and synthesize with it. The synthesis has not yet occurred. It is seen that within a period of three to four months there will be a change in the rotational pattern of this molecular structure in order to gear it up, so to speak, for these higher frequencies and other energies to begin. It's like it will set up a magnetic field of attraction at that point, and it will draw into itself the beginning stages of this energy which will be just the very beginning part of this synthesis.

Dr. Fuqua: Is this like a soul braid?

Athor: Very likely.

Later Athor again confirmed that this young man was in the preparation state for a soul braiding. It would take three to four years for the energies to completely merge. David kept in touch and returned for additional Athor readings over the next year. Each time the energy would be stronger. However, David was having extreme difficulty just coping with everyday life. Making a living was his main challenge, but going through all the emotional turmoil created by these kinds of experiments made him think at times that he was going insane. He would literally curl up on the floor when much of this kundalini type energy was entering his body. The last I heard of David he was living with a woman twice his age. He was slowly gaining confidence in himself since she is a spiritual woman who seems to really understand David. They appear to be a totally loving, devoted couple.

After David had his Athor reading, his mother requested a reading for herself. She also seemed quite unusual to me. Mother of eleven children, she seemed quite young and pretty. Apparently coping with all those children did not seem to greatly bother her although her husband had many difficulties and was little help at home. Athor discovered that David's mother was a Soul Braid herself, but this had happened to her at a much younger age. Because she had experienced many Earth incarnations herself prior to this lifetime, the Soul Braid experiment was much easier for her. It may be the reason for her rather detached attitude toward everything here on Earth. Later I heard through David that his mother, Paulette (not real name) had finally left her husband and seemed to be doing much better.

The totally fascinating part about these two cases is that Paulette in her reading asked about some of her children. It seems that at least two of her other children will also be Soul Braids when they are older; therefore, this seems to perhaps run in families.

Prior to working with David I had never heard of Soul Braids, but synchronistically, I had a telephone call from a woman in Sacramento who had earlier discussed her Walk-In experience with me. She knew of my work with Walk-Ins and told me I should know more about Soul Braids since she had finally determined that this was her particular type experiment. Due to our mutual busy schedules, we delayed getting together, but after I discovered that David was a Soul Braid, I immediately called Kadea Metara to set up a time for her to come to my office for a hypnosis session to get more details about this interesting phenomenon. We ended up with 50 pages of transcript. Kadea Metara's Soul Braid experiment began in 1976 after a near death experience in an automobile accident. Kadea later had an Athor reading that confirmed the fact that she is a Soul Braid. The following is her description of a Soul Braid from part of the transcript:

I am an embodied eleventh Elohim. The Elohim are the creator gods that hold the divine blueprint. The people that handle the soul braids are designed to hold these templates and this high vibration. Because there was such a problem integrating the soul braids most people either go crazy or commit suicide. There are only 25 people on the planet who have survived this experiment.

Dr. Fuqua: How long has this experiment been going on?

Kadea: From what they told me I was part of the original experiment. In 1975 when I had my accident is when they started preparing me.

Dr. Fuqua: From what I understand there have been so-called Walk-In experiments throughout the history of the Earth, but I gather the Soul Braid experiment is something new.

Kadea: Yes, this is new. It is not exactly like two souls in one body. You cannot call the Elohim a soul, you see. It is a vibrational frequency, an eleventh dimensional consciousness that carries out the divine plan. This frequency has not been able to be accessed before this time because of the lower vibrations of the etheric body. The planet was too dense. They picked certain Beings who had agreed before incarnation to come down here and anchor this frequency so that the density could be lifted from the entire planet. So this experiment is of the utmost importance for humanity and for the spiritual hierarchy. What is happening on the planet is called the Externalization of the Hierarchy. What is happening with this soul braiding is that the normal DNA structure has been distorted in the human species. The Elohim, Angels and Ascended Masters need to come and embody, which was not possible without doing this genetic engineering. So basically, it is a plan to get the builder gods that carry the divine plan into bodies. There are many Beings that have been prepared, all of the lifetimes they have ever been on this planet for this point in time to actually embody these energies, to be the living representatives of these frequencies, just as Jesus did, as well as the Buddha, Rama Krishna and others before Him.

Chapter 9
A Soul Exchange as an Adult

Dee Allen and her mate attended a lecture given by Athor and myself at the Sacramento Expo in late 1994. It was after hearing our talk that both of them began to wonder if they were some kind of Walk-In experiment. Dee came for an Athor reading in April of 1995 for clarification of her particular case.

Dr. Fuqua: Please give the exact date when you think the old soul left the body?

Dee: August 19, 1993

Athor: We have here a most peculiar image. What is the name you are now using?

Dee: Dee Janet Allen (fictitious name)

Athor: This appears to be a somewhat different procedure than the one that occurred to the body here on the couch (meaning the Athor body). It appears to have taken place in a semiconscious state. There was indeed an exchange. There are two individual soul lights which were exchanged.

Dee: I would like to know where the soul originated from.

Athor: We have here a scene; there is a spaceship, and there are some beings on the ship. It appears that your particular soul was infused through an interspecies exchange. Your soul, it appears, has had experiences as a so-called hybrid, being part human and parts of some other species. The exchange occurred through the medium of the ship, and your soul light was beamed down from a ship. It is seen that the other being was taken. The exchange that occurred is like your soul light came through from a spaceship so you had a type of form that was animate, but then the soul light left that form to take this form and the other soul left and was taken to

35

your beings. It is interesting because that does not always occur in an exchange. We will trace this back. The experience your soul has had has been of a hybrid type of existence. You are one of a growing number of beings that have been hybridized, one might say, for the purpose of strengthening not only the species that you came from but the beings on Earth as well. You are sort of a stepping stone, a midway link between two species.

Dr. Fuqua: What do you mean by her beings? Who are her beings?

Athor: The beings of the civilization that she came from, the Orion system. It was as if her soul reached a level where it wasn't just simply frustrated and wanted to get out and move on. It had reached a point from past cycles where it was ready to go on into this other existence, where this soul came from. The exchange was very interesting in that way because in Dee's case, the soul was released and it went on its way. It is seen that the soul has gone on into your star system.

Dr. Fuqua: When did these two souls make the agreement to make this exchange?

Athor: This is a very different type of experience. The other soul went into your star system because this is part of the entire experiment. What is involved here is more than just the removal of one soul light from a physical form into another and an exchange. What is involved is a much grander experiment of two souls, and there is something slated for perhaps a soul braiding at a later date between these two souls. It is not simply in your case that the other soul just left and it has gone on its merry way. It is still part of the experiment. There will be at a future date a reconnection of some type between these two souls. There is some kind of advance work being done here. It is another unique experiment on a soul level which is occurring here.

Dr. Fuqua: At what point did the two souls make an agreement for this experiment?

Athor: This was done through the existence in that system. It is seen that the other soul had other cycles. Although many were on Earth, it had other cycles in other systems in passing so to speak. There is a level of recognition between these two soul lights which we do not believe has yet dawned on the Being. Your particular soul light has had some Earth cycles so it is not like this was a first time for you. You seem to have developed a knack of functioning on the Earth plane level perhaps due to the fact that the vehicle which you entered had made preparation for your entry.

Dr. Fuqua: How did the soul energy come into Dee's body?

Athor: That is difficult to say because the nature of the exchange was not done in a fully conscious state, and so as a consequence of this, we see the energy blending in through the back and coming into not simply one chakra but like an osmosis process of coming through the entire back of the body and coming around and through the vehicle. The other soul consciousness had withdrawn its energies from the chakra systems. It had accumulated all the energies in the various chakra systems and brought it all together into what might be termed a ball of energy or light. It was sitting out here somewhere in the auric field, but it had already withdrawn all its cords and connections into this ball of energy so that when the present soul began to come through, the other one was simply a ball of light that went up. Your soul light came in through all the chakras almost simultaneously. It was a diffusion method almost. During the process the cord was not disconnected. It was simply reconnected to this present soul.

Dr. Fuqua: Did the exchange take place here on Earth or was the body beamed up to a spaceship?

Athor: No, it occurred here on Earth, but the other being had to come down from the ship.

Dee: I've had many physical problems. Is this the karma of the outgoing soul or my soul?

Athor: I hear both. About two-thirds of it is what was left by the out-going soul, and then there is a slight residue of your own.

Dr. Fuqua: This reading is greatly condensed. It includes only the facts that might be of interest to the readers. As with all Walk-Ins, this is a difficult experiment. Dee's health problems are on-going although her consciousness has evolved by leaps and bounds since I first met Dee. Along with soul Braids it would seem that soul exchanges are probably the most difficult of all of these so-called Walk-In experiments. Perhaps this is due to the tremendous difference in vibration between the two souls.

Chapter 10
A Different Kind of Near Death Experience

Nan was in an automobile accident in 1967. Severely injured, she was placed in intensive care for nine days during which time she was in a coma. The doctors thought she would never walk again so were amazed that she could get up and walk out of the hospital. At this point she felt totally detached from her family. She had many feelings of being quite different after her experience in the hospital. She had assumed that she probably was a Walk-In. Can you give clarification as to what really happened?

Athor: What we see here is that the consciousness of this being was removed. It left. It is an unusual situation because it did not leave entirely. There was not an actual complete transference as such. What we are seeing is that the consciousness or the soul essence left and was healed in a sense. But this was not your typical so-called healing.

There was some kind of a situation that occurred in the transitional phase where the being's consciousness went into another dimensional frequency; perhaps what might be termed extraterrestrial where some kind of beings worked on the being itself. The consciousness of this being did indeed return, but it returned in an altered state because much had been done to both the etheric vehicles and the astral bodies as well. There was some type of an experimentation in which the being was healed, but it was more than that. There were certain infusions which were made, certain additions, one might say. We see a surgical procedure that occurred in the other realms in which the being itself was surgically transmuted and became quite different in a sense. There were certain elements, a certain vibratory frequency, which we see was withdrawn from this being. Others were infused.

39

The emotional nature was altered considerably, due in part to the accident, but more due to the changes which occurred and which were produced in this transmutation process. There were some unusual surgical procedures performed on this being on the other side, and we see that the being in the time it remained in the so-called comatose state, was indeed being operated on in the other levels as we see that the beings who did this were beings with which this one, Nan, had some contact and connection in previous cycles. They wished her to be able to remain in a body and to continue on with her learning process.

We see that certain emotional frequencies were removed from this being's psyche and consciousness. This is in part what makes this being feel at times that perhaps she is a little odd or different or perhaps even cold at times; yet that is not the quality that we see. We see there is a great deal of compassion within this being and a great deal of healing energy which has been able to channel through the being.

Dr. Fuqua: Can you get some more information on what experience Nan had with these extraterrestrials in past existences?

Athor: We have here a scene wherein there is a humanoid being that looks less humanoid than humans do. This being only has three fingers, and it appears that the foot structure is quite different. There appear to be three toes. This being is somewhat large but of small build. It has a large head, large eyes, and in a one-piece suit which is extremely tight fitting to the skin. These beings, when they manifest in a type of physical density are very sensitive to many of the physical elements. They wear these protective suits that are like a second skin.

The being is coming towards Nan's being and is handing her something. It appears they are both of the same structure. The entity here today takes this object which is somewhat like a computer chip that goes into a device in the ship. It is seen that a star map appears of several galactic systems. There is one star in particular that lights up. This is the information that this being needed because it was some type of space travel. They were on some kind of exploratory mapping mission where they went to different star systems and checked in on various locations to see what type of life forms were indeed present in those places. This being here today was on the craft and as this one area lit up, it traveled there. It is now out in space in this craft. It is a small craft with only two other beings. The three of them are supposed to explore this star system, map it, etc.

It is seen that there is some type of magnetic force field that comes up. There is an interdimensional, we hear time warp factor that came on rather suddenly. This was an area they had not charted before so consequently when this occurred, they weren't prepared. They didn't have the means to deal with it so it is seen that the craft was sucked into this magnetic field, and the structure of the ship itself was completely disintegrated. There was tremendous pressure that caused an implosion rather than an explosion. The craft just split apart from within into thousands of particles.

It is seen that the beings on the ship for some reason did not implode. They were trapped in the field itself. It is seen they were sucked into some energy configuration vortex which was completely unknown to them. Basically, they lingered there for eons. Of course, in that time period, the consciousness animating those forms had left by then because the forms themselves were not destroyed for a very long period of time.

The being had to experience leaving a form that was no longer functional. The beings that centered on that mission are also the beings that came and did these surgical healing methods on this being in this lifetime. They could not help it in that lifetime because this was so far beyond their consciousness and comprehension that they just had no idea how to deal with it (the implosion as described). This time there was something they could do because they were concerned. There is a great bond here between these beings because of this one having been of that race, and so basically they watch over her. They try to help and take care of her when they can. They are, of course, limited in certain respects, but they do the best they can. There is a bond of love and loyalty and kinship.

Dr. Fuqua: Can you identify the home star system of these beings?

Athor: They are in the Andromeda system.

Dr. Fuqua: What else can you tell us about Nan that will help her understand her sudden transformational experience?

Athor: This is not a Walk-In; this is not an experiment. The beings were motivated by love and compassion.

There are many, many beings on the face of this Earth today that have many ideas about what occurred to them in cases of sudden transformation of personality. If we look at an overview of those who consider themselves to be so-called Walk-Ins, we would say that approximately 30 percent of them are indeed in the category of some type of soul exchange. You and others would like to know in a neat little category what happened to the remaining 70 percent. That is not possible. We deal with each individual case. In giving you this overview, that approximately 30 percent of them are indeed soul exchanges; that should give you an idea that it is not as frequent as some would have you believe.

Dr. Fuqua: This indeed is consistent with our research. Each reading of a so-called Walk-In has been unique.

Chapter 11
The Moon and the Secret Government

Dr. Fuqua: Can you give us some information about the moon?

Athor: The moon itself has had three layers of life forms. There was the outermost layer, then the middle, then the innermost layer within the core of the moon itself. There were varying times in which all three layers were populated by beings of various types as well as times in which only one or two layers were populated. So this is why you have a larger percentage of beings from the moon because it supported a great deal of life forms. (See chapter 6 Destruction of Maldek).

Dr. Fuqua: Were these life forms in the various layers each quite different? (Athor is speaking of life forms that are indigenous to the moon).

Athor: Yes.

Dr. Fuqua: Are there any life forms on the moon today?

Athor: Not in the physical form. Within the moon itself there is an etheric layer, but it is not physical.

Dr. Fuqua: Are the stories of the astronauts actually seeing spacecraft on the moon true?

Athor: That does not mean that these craft actually came from the moon per se.

Dr. Fuqua: Are there presently any space stations on the moon?

Athor: We do not see any life forms per se. We do see some type of relay apparatus. It is for this reason that many of the satellite systems have been set up. It would have required various relay stations along the way.

Dr. Fuqua: Are these relay stations owned by the U.S. Government?

Athor: By a certain phase of the government, but not by the country as a whole. They are owned by the so-called 'secret government'.

Dr. Fuqua: Would you elaborate on the 'secret government'.

Athor: Let's put it this way. There has been much written about your so-called 'secret government'. We would say that approximately 35% of what is written is accurate. (No further comments from Athor regarding this question).

Chapter 12
Child from Orion

Many parents in their quest to understand their children have requested Athor readings for them. It was after I had conducted a regression for a nine year old child that I turned to Athor to get confirmation about information coming from the child in this regression.

When I began the regression with Anandara she did not go into a past life but insisted that she had been an angel. She talked about the colors they wore, and girl and boy angels. She said that in order to have crowns they have to come to Earth. She also said she is the guardian angel for her baby brother.

Anandara had long blonde hair with delicate features. I could well imagine that she had come from the Angelic kingdom since we have learned that angels do occasionally incarnate here on Earth. However, when I asked Athor about this child, she said that her most recent existence was on another constellation, Orion. She lived in a very beautiful city similar to our concept of the Garden of Eden. She had visited the Earth a few times in other life forms for brief periods prior to this incarnation Athor's explanation as to why Anandara thought she had been an angel was because in the child's experience that was the only form anywhere close to what she remembers on Orion. When asked about Anandara's connection to her baby brother, Athor replied that the two of them had been together on Orion. Since this was not a full reading, I did not attempt to get greater details, but this explains why Anandara seems to be so greatly affected by the dense vibrations of the Earth. Her most recent past life memories were of her beautiful and peaceful 'city' on Orion.

This case brings to mind a child about the same age who attended the elementary school where I was a counselor. She too looked like an angel with long blonde hair and a wonderfully sweet personality. However, school was quite a problem to her and her family. She frequently would get severe stomach aches and have to go home during the school day. It was my theory at the time (before having Anandara as a client) that the noisy vibrations of her classroom were having a physical effect on this very delicate child. My school had many acting out children which resulted in temper tantrums, etc. that could easily have affected the quieter, shy children in the classrooms. In talking to the parents of the child, we all agreed that Sharon (not real name) probably was recently of ET origins and finding it very difficult to cope with the dense vibrations here on Earth. While having them understand the root of the problem, Sharon felt less like something was wrong with her so seemed to adjust somewhat better to school.

Chapter 13
Past Lives as an Extraterrestrial

Anthony (a fictitious name to insure confidentiality) is a well-known inventor who is president and owner of his own company. He had numerous Athor readings over the years. Anthony is well educated, extremely spiritual, and well-read in the metaphysical field. It is partly because of Anthony's belief in the validity of the Athor readings that inspired me to produce a newsletter and eventually to write a book about the Athor saga. Anthony has given me permission to use portions of two of his particularly interesting readings.

Dr. Fuqua: Anthony's first question: "Why do we have On-Earth experiences versus Off-Earth? Do Off-Earth experiences proceed On-Earth or is Off-Earth primarily a between On-Earth experience? What is the relative importance of On-Earth versus Off-Earth experiences? (We had established the fact in earlier readings that Anthony has had many Off-Earth as well as numerous On-Earth experiences).

Athor: All cycles, whether they be in physical incarnation or as you would term it 'in between' are simply for the soul to experience certain things. There are certain areas such as in the physical where certain experiences only can be experienced which cannot be experienced to that degree in non-physical realities. So basically there is no particular order as such in that a soul first has 'x' amount of earth incarnations and then 'x' amount of other types of cycles, but rather simply that they are expressions of that soul light which wishes to both experience, experiment and also to give of itself in a particular realm. So it is a multifaceted experience, regardless of whether it is in the physical realm or in Off-Earth existences. There is no linear order as such, no so-called logical sequence to incarnations whether physical or non-physical.

Dr. Fuqua: So a person could have 'x' number of Earth experiences and then go to Off-Earth, then back to Earth?

Athor: Yes. There are many who have experiences in the physical incarnation and then they go in between to Off-Earth existences, and return to physical incarnations. It is not a simple matter that you have 'x' amount of physical incarnations and you finish. To a certain degree there is an element of that, but it is not an amount but rather how much experience it has acquired, and whether it has balanced out its debits and credits, so to speak. That is the matter of the physical incarnations. The Off-Earth existences do not have the karmic consequences in the manner in which physical existences do. There is a certain matter of being somewhat 'locked in' to the physical once a certain round of cause and effect has been established through the physical. So perhaps in that sense there is a certain limitation in a certain order perhaps in which the being must complete but yet can still have Off-Earth existences in between the physical incarnations, but the soul then again returns to manifest physically if it has not finished the cycle of debits and credits on the physical plane.

Dr. Fuqua: Our research on readings has shown that you said there is no karma in the Off-Earth kind of existences, but it would indicate that if two souls had experiences together Off-Earth that can have a profound effect upon the individuals if they meet again on the Earth plane.

Athor: Yes, it is not the karma as you know of on the physical plane. To use the word 'karma' is not perhaps appropriate in that sense. The effect is very much there, but that only comes into play because of the greater number of vehicles through the physical realm incarnations. So if a being has had Off-Earth existences and has met another soul entity, and then they end up eventually in a physical plane incarnation, the effect of that meeting is extremely intense because of the added vehicles that are present through a physical plane incarnation. So there are more avenues of expression than in the non-physical realms.

Dr. Fuqua: When you speak of added vehicles do you mean chakras?

Athor: Yes.

Dr. Fuqua: Let's go to Anthony's second question. What was his most recent Off-Earth experience?

Athor: We are having difficulty in what is being seen. We will attempt to explain. This so far is only a realm of energies. We do not see any particular forms, but rather energies. They translate into certain light, but that is not really consequential. Now we are going into a strange type of inter-dimensional tunnel type thing, and at the end of this telescopic type vision, we see a rather dark place. It does not have light from a sun but rather it is dimmer. It has a silvery light about it, but it isn't very bright so it is kind of a muted twilight type of place. For some reason it is difficult to find this particular being there. There is a small type of being on the surface of this place which does not appear to be the Anthony being. It is a rather curious looking thing, and it is moving about on the surface of this place. This creature is partly mechanical and partly sentient, and it's sort of moving on this place like a spider, but also like those caterpillar machines. It is taking samples from the surface of the place. Through its legs it sucks in the samples. The thing returns to a base, and there are several beings there. These beings do not have hair or any facial hair. They seem to be more of your 'cone head' type structure. They have a peculiar bluish — violet light that emanates from the top of the head where it comes to a peak.

There is an aura of this bluish-violet-white light. Evidently that light seems to indicate that these are sentient beings, and it is of that particular race, whereas the creature was an entirely different type of mechanism. One of these beings appears to be you. Each of these beings has a very specific function in this place. You are obtaining data about the place to see if it can be colonized and if it can bring forth certain substances that are necessary for your particular group. It would seem that there is some disagreement among the members as to certain calculations.

There seems to be some great importance about these calculations because it has to do with the survival of that species. There is a kind of tension involved with these calculations and their accuracy. Since there is disagreement among the group, it is seen that one of the people has to take the brunt of it. They cannot come back with five or ten different theories and calculations and so forth. There is a meeting, and many of these beings sit down to share their particular observations. Whether it was up to you or whether you took that on or it was agreed you would take it on is not certain, but it was left to you to determine the exact factors. You are pouring over the various data that had been collected, and it was a real puzzlement and seemed to be a real difficulty for you because something about the various calculations. You pondered and pondered. This was more involved with physical, not physical to the extent of what it is on Earth, but a more physical type of data rather than simply etheric type of data. This was a place not similar to Earth in a sense of atmospheric conditions, etc. but the fact there was a greater density than in some other Off-Earth times. It seems that the image just stays where you are just pondering this. You took this information back, but you had not been able to synthesize all of it, so you had to take some of the individual ones back in their entirely rather than synthesizing the data as a whole. You conferred with some other beings. There seems to be a strong feeling of 'this has to be it'. There was a difficulty about putting that data together, and we do not have the full picture, but it had to do with the data that was required to see if the life forms could be supported. We feel that the problem was kind of left hanging. There was a feeling in your psyche, Anthony, of resignation, but also lack of fulfillment. In a sense some of that translated into your Earthly existence, into your present day cycle of wishing to make things happen in physical realms, to procure certain advancements. So this is part of that whole scenario because you were not fulfilled in that existence quite the way you would have liked.

Dr. Fuqua: Did this happen on a planet we might recognize?

Athor: It was one of those in the Andromeda system.

Dr. Fuqua: It would appear that we have Off-Earth experiences which vary in density.

Athor: Yes. There can be Off-Earth physical experiences, but they do not necessarily have to be physical. There is not a logical sequence at all times. It is again dependent on that particular soul and its cycles and choices.

Dr. Fuqua: Part of Anthony's question is "What was his most important Off-Earth experience?" I don't know if you can quantify these Off-Earth experiences, but do you have any answer to that?

Athor: Important in terms of what?

Anthony: (I conducted readings but when the clients were present they occasionally want to clarify a particular question). I suppose in terms of either self-accomplishment or general accomplishment - perhaps something I had done that was useful to other people or me. Are there varying degrees of Off-Earth experiences in terms of what they teach us or what we may teach other people or other things depending on what's going on? Maybe I'm trying to quantify the Off-Earth experience in too specific a way.

Athor: Each cycle whether it be physical on the Earth plane or elsewhere or non-physical is in one way basically an entity unto itself. There is a carryover because that soul experiences these cycles A, B, C, etc. On one level from the soul standpoint, each one is an entity unto itself and therefore is equally important to any of the other cycles that the particular soul has experienced. The manner in which you would like to quantify this answer is one that is coming from the logical mind rather than looking at the spiritual aspect of the entire picture. In looking at the entire soul picture, there is not one particular life cycle that is any more important than another.

Anthony: Let me rephrase the question: Which one of those Off-Earth cycles might be most significant in terms of my present one because I certainly appreciate what you just said. In the broad sense, that every one is just as important, but there may be one that had more significance to where I am at the moment.

Athor: We have here a scene in which there is some type of flying craft. There appears to be, we're not certain if it's a skirmish, there's a lot of activity. There is testing and flying and things of that sort. As the flying craft comes down various people get out. It's almost like the Air Force. The beings are the vanguard leaders of this group of beings. They are sort of the Guardians, the soldiers that patrol and keep track of the perimeters of various areas of Space. They come back and they are debriefed by this one being who seems to be your general or someone like that on Earth. One of the pilots is having some difficulty with this 'general' being and decides that he is going to try out something different and go on to another sector. As a result that being hits a force field in that area of space. We don't know if it was generated or simply out there. The craft and all on board were disintegrated. The general, who appears to be you, Anthony, was very distraught. It appears that this pilot was one of the beings whom you have many dealings with in this life cycle. There was nothing that could be done because the being had taken it on himself to do this. There appears to be a feeling within your psyche of not having done enough, of not being able to complete, of wanting to put it all together; to make it all work. This is a very deep underlying feeling within this being's psyche which has stemmed from other existences wherein it has not worked in the manner in which you had hoped for. Though this was not in any way your doing nor your fault, you took it upon yourself because you felt responsible for this group of beings, since you were in a sense their leader. We see the deep pondering again and turning deep within. It is almost as though the being wishes to change the very nature of reality, of certain types of energies. We are not saying there is anything wrong with that, but what we are indicating is that feeling has assisted you on one hand in your pursuits in this cycle, in your inventions, in your ideas. That is an insatiable feeling.

From day one this particular being, the essence has been connected and concerned with energy. This is not simply limited to the Earth plane understanding of energy; it goes much beyond that. So there has always been this feeling of discontent that "Wait, it isn't enough, that's fine but we've got to go on, there is more and more and more." Again we are not putting a negative connotation on this because it has actually been a positive asset to you in your work. You are never quite satisfied with any one device, any one invention. There is always more. Is that not the case?

Anthony: Yes, I appreciate that. That's excellent, thank you.

Chapter 14
Past Lives of Jesus

Al Holcomb was a very interesting man who drove from New York State to have some therapy sessions with me and to have several Athor readings. Al had been an attorney, and then later in life had a series of kundalini experiences. He had a strong Christian background but also believed in reincarnation. After having a session with me in which Al gave a long description of a lifetime when he was a follower of Jesus, he wanted to follow up with an Athor reading to see if what he was 'remembering' was accurate. As always Athor had no knowledge of Al or his regression prior to her reading. The following are excerpts from that reading.

Dr. Fuqua: Can you provide more details about how Al came to know Jesus during the time when Jesus was on Earth?

Athor: We have here a scene where there are two male beings walking along a dusty road. Both of them are carrying a staff. They are having a discussion as they are walking. Every once in a while some kind of animal runs into the roadway, and they have to make it get out of their way which is part of the reason for their carrying staffs. One is dressed in what appears to be a monk's habit of some type, not a robe, but typical of the dress of that time. The other man is bare-chested and appears to have strange marks on the skin on his chest. It is almost as if this being has been sacrificing his body, flagellating himself, or at least it appears that way as we see it. These marks appear to be scars of one sort or another.

These two are talking as they walk along, but it is difficult to tune into exactly what they are saying. They are speaking about going to see a teacher, a holy man who preached and has gathered many beings around him. They are discussing the pros and cons of certain principles - a religious type discussion.

The one who is bare-chested falls into a depression in the road, injuring his foot and ankle badly. It does not appear that the bone was broken, but there is damage to the tendons and ligaments. It is quite a severe injury. The other one is helping him walk, holding his arm around his shoulder to support him as they walk along.

At length they come to the foot of a mountain where a man is up toward the top with many people gathered around who are sitting down and listening as he speaks. He is speaking about his Father, and these types of things. These two men, having arrived late, are sitting on the outer area of the crowd of people. They have difficulty hearing so every once in a while they ask people around them what he is saying. They gradually move closer up because they cannot hear well, and they have a great desire to hear what this teacher is saying. They find themselves hanging on every word, so they keep moving closer as opportunities present themselves.

As they get within a certain perimeter of this teacher, the one who is bare-chested finds that his leg is completely healed. The pain is gone, and he can step on it and walk. So he immediately is most impressed. This is the same entity (Al) here today seeking this information. He bowed down and was most worshipful to this unusual man because he sees and feels that as the result of entering the energy field of this Jesus, the healing occurred. He becomes almost mesmerized, and this was the beginning of the spark of consciousness, the soul-awareness of this individual. Not that he had no interest in these matters before, but it was not of soul consciousness up until this occurrence. It was simply more of an intellectual understanding.

These matters had been the subject under discussion by the two men as they had journeyed to listen to this Jesus teach. So, this entity had an instantaneous revelation on the spot when his leg was healed. He became in a sense transfigured because for the first time ever in all the cycles he had had he achieved oneness with the soul consciousness of the Christ. It was a completely mind and life altering experience for this being at that time. It is seen that this entity paid heed and followed where this one Jesus went, and just went from place to place where this one Jesus taught and spoke.

It is not seen that at this time he became one of the inner circle around Jesus, so to speak, but it was close enough wherein there was a very gradual and great energy exchange which took place from the heart of this Jesus to the heart and soul of this entity here with us today.

It could be said that there was an energy-bonding and this entity has a deep, deep love for the Christ being. It is an overwhelming sense that fills his heart because it was through this Christ being that the Light of the soul first came into him. As it was for many in that day and time, for many beings on the face of this planet at that time had lost that link and that consciousness. Many had totally 'fallen asleep', spiritually speaking and they were no longer aware that there was such a thing as God or even that there was such a thing as a soul or that the two had a connection with each other.

Many different teachings in that day taught of material pleasures and sensory delights being of predominant importance so that these beings had become further and further removed from Soul consciousness. There was indeed no Light which was present for those beings on Earth who had lost contact and connection. There were some who had managed to preserve their soul-consciousness despite what was occurring around them, but they lived in communities by themselves primarily because they saw that in that time the other beings had lost sight of these things or perhaps many of them had never yet gained it. These became steeped further and further in this great materialistic illusion. So those beings that still had that remnant of Light left within their souls chose to isolate themselves from the others who were in spiritual darkness.

The being Jesus came forth to the multitudes for it was the multitudes that had lost the spiritual Light and had lost the awareness and the link with their soul Light. This was what might be termed a mass infusion of Light which this being Jesus came to offer, because the greater part of the population were in danger of losing all connection to their spirit souls. Many were so far gone into darkness that something had to occur in order to bring forth the next phase so the spiritual seeds would not die out. It was for this reason that the Christ essence came forth as the being Jesus, manifesting its Light to renew that spark in all of these beings, in all their souls, for they had indeed lost sight of their heavenly connection.

Al: Were the Essenes one of these groups who remained apart from others?

Athor: Yes.

Dr. Fuqua: Did Jesus live first on Earth as Adam?

Athor: Yes.

Dr. Fuqua: Did he live next as Enoch?

Athor: Yes.

Dr. Fuqua: Was he on Earth as Melchizedek, priest of the Most High God in heavenly planes?

Athor: Yes.

Dr. Fuqua: Did he incarnate as Joseph, son of Jacob to lead the Hebrews into Egypt in fulfillment of the promise the Lord made to Abraham?

Athor: Yes.

Dr. Fuqua: Did he incarnate as Joshua, son of Nun, who was selected by God to take the Israelites across Jordan as a sign to them of his heavenly powers to save them?

Athor: Yes.

Dr. Fuqua: Did he incarnate as Asaph in David's time?

Athor: Yes.

Dr. Fuqua: Did he incarnate as Joshua, son of Josedech, high priest who came out of the 70 year exile with Zerubbabel to rebuild the temple and Jerusalem?

Athor: Yes.

Dr. Fuqua: Did he incarnate last as Jesus of Nazareth, thereby completing his Earth cycles, having fulfilled his Earth missions?

Athor: Yes.

Dr. Fuqua: In what form may we expect the Christ to reappear after tribulations are finished to usher in the coming New Age Millennium?

Athor: He will reappear in the form of what might be best termed the 'Christ-Essence' which is the energy which will become manifested in each and every being who has allowed that spark to revivify their soul consciousness. The Christ being is not simply limited to a form per se, as opposed to any other form. This is a human understanding that he may take a particular form when He returns. (Jesus was known as Jesus the Christ but the terms are not synonymous).

Dr. Fuqua: Did this entity (Al) witness the events at Gethsemane and Golgotha, and was he present at the crucifixion?

Athor: He was present at Gethsemane and Golgotha, but not at the site of the Crucifixion until late, almost the next day. This being traveled in what might be called the circuits established by Jesus, always present, mostly in the fringes of the crowds, but not necessarily taking any active role other than accompanying the followers. He learned much which he carries today.

Dr. Fuqua: Can you describe Christ's position in the 'All That Is"?

Athor: The Christ-Essence is a direct energy ray which has come forth from the Logos. The Logos of this system, this universe, is one differentiated aspect of the "All That Is'. The Christ-Essence is the direct ray coming forth from the Logos, animating all the souls which have emanated from that Logos. The Christ-Essence has what might be termed an individualized ray connecting or linking it to all souls which have come forth from that Logos. In other universes, there are other expressions and experiences. The Christ-Essence is of this universe alone.

Dr. Fuqua: How many universes are there altogether?

Athor: Seventeen.

Note by Dr. Fuqua: Amazingly, Al had accurately 'remembered' most of this in his regressions with me. The history of the incarnations of Jesus was based on Al's study of the Edgar Cayce material and other research in spiritual teachings. He felt this was 'truth' but he wanted Athor's verification.

Al did not ask about this, but Jesus ascended and became an Ascended Master who goes by the name of Sananda.

The Christ-Essence is different from the physical Jesus being.

Chapter 15
Closing Thoughts

I have chosen to make this a short book since the material may require some pondering to understand. Often after a reading I would think of many questions which I would have liked to ask, but the Athor readings were limited to one hour due to the energy drain on Rose-Athor's body. Afterward she completely forgot about what she had said, but she could readily pick up on a client's soul records if they returned for follow-up readings as was the case with Anthony who had dozens of readings over the years when I was in the Rocklin area.

Considering the history of the Earth and all of the experimenting on the human form to get to where we are today in the evolution of the Earth, one could take a very pessimistic view of humanity. However, we can rest assured that the All That Is (aka God) is overseeing all of the universes and we are all expressions of the All That Is. If we continually incorporate 'Light' into our psyches, we begin to realize what a grand and glorious experiment the human race can be. God has many helpers in the realms of Light that are giving us much assistance in moving safely into a higher vibration. Namaste!

The Wisdom of Athor
Book Two

Evelyn Fuqua Ph.D.

O.M.R.A.
Bandon, Oregon
2013

Readings from the Akashic Records by Athor, one member of the Council of Twelve on the Star System of Sirius

For information:
P.O. Box 341
Bandon, Oregon 97411
http://www.evelynfuqua.com

Acknowledgements

My deep appreciation to all of my clients who gave me permission to publish information from their soul readings; to my mate Paul for his loving support and continual computer assistance; to Michael Phelan for formatting the book for publication and to Athor for his/her wisdom which was extremely helpful to my clients and hopefully will be of assistance to my readers for their enlightenment.

May you always be surrounded by "The Light"

The "Light" is of a radiance and magnitude which far exceeds the human sensory apparatus. "The Light" is that energy which proceeds from an undifferentiated source.

It is your link to the Divine.

Table of Contents - Book Two

About the Author

Evelyn Fuqua holds a B.A. in Psychology from Agnes Scott College, an M.A. in counseling from California State University Sacramento and a Ph.D. in Psychology from the Professional School of Psychology. She was a teacher, resource specialist and counselor in the public schools for 33 years.

Dr. Fuqua served six years on the Board of Directors of the Association of Past Life Research and Therapy (presently International Association for Regression Research and Therapies). She was State Relations Chairman for the California State Counselors Association. Fuqua has presented numerous workshops at professional conferences.

After retiring from the school system, she was in private practice as a Marriage, Family Therapist specializing in past life regression therapy and working with clients who are "Walk-Ins" or who have had other ET experiences.

Dr. Fuqua is the author *of From Sirius to Earth: A Therapist Discovers a Soul Exchange, Cosmic Relationships: Exploring the Soul's Journey from Off-Earth, Earth Lives, and Reincarnation*, and *The Wisdom of Athor: Book One.*

Evelyn is currently enjoying retirement on the Oregon coast with her mate Paul and her cat Boots.

"Out yonder there is this huge world which exists independently of us human beings and which stands before us like a great, eternal riddle, at least partially accessible to our inspection and thinking."

~ Albert Einstein

Preface

In 1988 a woman named Rose came to my office for hypnotherapy, with the hope that I could "cure" her of environmental illness which was often life threatening.

Unfortunately that never happened. Instead, we discovered that she was an extraterrestrial, one member of the Council of Twelve from the star system Sirius. When she was three years, two months old the Athor soul overshadowed the Rose soul. For many years we thought this was an actual soul exchange, but finally in 2005 I discovered that the Athor soul had "walked out". This was a shock to all of us who personally knew her. The entire complicated story of Rose/Athor is chronicled in *From Sirius to Earth* with some additional information in *Cosmic Relationships*. Since the overshadowing occurred at such an early age, Rose took on the abilities and personality of Athor, feeling that she really was Athor; therefore, when Athor left, Rose was very confused and it has taken a while for her to adjust to her new vibrations. Her environmental illness continues and she is developing her own psychic abilities.

During the early days of Rose's therapy I became aware that she had a remarkable ability to read the Akashic records. After having her do numerous readings for myself and my husband, I finally decided to ask her to do readings for my clients after they had reached a certain point in their therapy. I also began a newsletter for my organization called O.M.R.A. (Oakdell Multidimensional Research Association). *Book One* of *The Wisdom of Athor* includes material published in our newsletter. *Book Two* of *The Wisdom of Athor* is based on the readings for my clients. As conductor for the readings, I asked questions that the clients gave to me before a session with Athor. I would also include questions I felt would assist the clients in understanding their "root" problem. The readings were very long, therefore, I have extrapolated certain portions that illustrate souls have much off-earth experiences before coming to earth. During the readings, Athor repeatedly asked for the name of the client. The name was the gateway to reading the soul's records. There were numerous times when Athor would pause and say "One moment please" before getting more information. This comment has been deleted to avoid a great deal of repetition.

After several years of working with Athor I realized that the material from her readings was knowledge that could help humankind evolve. We jointly wrote *From Sirius to Earth*. After the book was published people began writing to request readings, many from various parts of the United States and Canada. Some were able to attend the sessions in person but most were too far away to make that practical. We offered past life readings or readings from the Source (origin of soul). While the vast majority explored lives here on Earth, many were interested in readings from the Source, and those are the readings I am writing about in *Book Two*. At this point in time there have been many books written about past lives but none to my knowledge have discussed souls from their birth.

This material is quite in-depth and personal; therefore, no real names are used. Rose continues to be a fictitious name in order to protect her identity. She has never wanted to be a public figure. All of these readings were given by Athor before she/he left the Rose body. My comments and some questions by the clients who attended sessions in person are in italics; all other text is directly from the Athor readings, although some minor changes have been made for clarity.

As with *Cosmic Relationships*, my goal for the reader is to give an understanding that there is a Creator (All That Is) and there are many civilizations and dimensions that souls experience before coming to Earth. From my research I have found that souls evolve through inhabiting many different forms that are not human before incarnating here on Earth. Therefore, there is really no conflict between evolution and creationism. Everything in the universe is about creating and evolving.

In editing these readings to make them more understandable, I am repeatedly struck by the thought, "No one will believe this because it sounds so much like science fiction". That is okay! Believe only what feels true to your particular consciousness. Considering the many universes, star systems, etc. we all come to Earth open to certain belief systems, depending on our own past lives on and off Earth. I personally do not understand much of this since there appear to be what I think are quantum physics concepts; but as Athor advised to readers of *From Sirius to Earth,* just allow your mind to take in what it CAN understand. It was her opinion that just reading the book helps raise your awareness and vibrations. I hope the same is true of this book!

Chapter 1
Client with Fibromyalgia

Am I a star person?

It is seen that this being was brought here to this planet in an attempt to help colonize this planet Earth. There seems to be a difficulty surrounding that initial beginning upon this Earth plane. When this being arrived upon this plane this being was not entirely desirous of residing upon this planet. However, it had been decided by those you might say "higher up" from the particular sphere wherein she originally resided that this being would be one of many to colonize a certain part of the Earth plane. There is much darkness surrounding this particular entry in that time as it did not wholeheartedly wish to be transported here. It was almost as though there was a split within the being and because she was part of the plan, so to speak, in this particular colonization, she went along with it. But there resides yet in the memory bank a strong aversion to the physical plane dimension which has as yet not been resolved. It is seen that the being had a certain capacity on the star system from which it came, but her planet was in the throes of destruction. There are yet lingering feelings and emotions of the time before this Earth when the being did not suffer, as the density was not of this same frequency and there was less physicality and a different type of physical structure as it allowed for a greater degree of mobility of the physical vehicle. This being was used to being more unencumbered, as it were, and still deeply yearns for that state of so-called unencumbered state. That state was one of what would be termed complete spiritual alignment, wherein all the auric bodies are totally harmonized and balanced, so if the being spends much time and energy in seeking this spiritual alignment and balancing, rather than yearning for that which it seems to have lost, then that is the goal which the soul has chosen in this life cycle will indeed be fulfilled, though it is seen that this being will once again return, if not to the physical plane dimension, to one of a similar frequency for it is seen that the being has a great desire to be of assistance, to aid and assist those around her. It is this quality and this desire which will bring this being back into a type of incarnation process wherein she will then be able to be the guidance and the teaching force, the torch light she yet yearns and seeks to become.

Could you identify the planet that was destroyed?

It is a planet which is approximately 30 billion light years from your solar galaxy. There is difficulty in energy frequency, as you see when you are dealing with star systems which are so far removed from this galactic system. The energy frequency is so different that when you are tapping into that frequency there will be disturbances to your electrical system. *(Several tape recordings did not record in some readings about Off-Earth existences).*

Will you scan the physical body and determine what is causing the fibromyalgia?

The original source was a split of the being not wishing to colonize here. You might say there was a certain homesickness present when the being was transported here, and there was a great sadness as her planetary sphere was in the process of being destroyed. So this sadness lingered with the being when it was brought to this planetary sphere. There is a certain level of disassociation; it is this dislike and inner rejection of the physical plane dimension that has created a very strong current of destructiveness within the physical atoms and molecules.

As a therapist dealing with many clients deep into metaphysics, there seemed to be a large number of people

2

suffering from fibromyalgia. Many of them had a similar off-Earth background that for various reasons they really didn't want to be here on Earth in a physical body. The exact circumstances varied but the underlying theme seemed to be they really didn't want to be here. This particular client later went through an experience wherein her Higher Self came into her psyche which resulted in a much more positive mental outlook. While she still has fibromyalgia, she is better able to cope with her physical problems.

Chapter 2
An Adventurous Soul

Please go into George's off-Earth existences.

We have here a scene in what one might almost term the little green men. The being we are viewing has a rather solid frame. It does not appear to be of any type of ectoplasm. It appears rather solid. It indeed appears to have a greenish tinge to the skin and appears to be somewhat amphibious in nature from the appearance of it. It might have been an off shoot of one of the other races which was not directly from the reptilian core. We see that the being is a young being in that system. It has not matured yet. It is very mischievous and just wanted to learn about everything similar to some Earth children who are very curious, inquisitive, etc.

We see that as the being matured, the appearance also changed considerably because it was no longer like a little green man but grew into an androgynous looking being that still had the same type of skin but was much taller, and actually the coloring changes as these beings mature. It changes from that greenish tinge to a more muted bluish, grayish tinge. These were some of the forerunners that were from the Andromeda strain, and they were placed in various systems and on various stars to both do scientific research and to colonize certain systems as well. This particular being was one of those who was sent to planets to colonize. So he came with a big group of those beings and they were searching for the life forms upon this plane. Once they found them, they were to mingle with them and learn their ways and try to achieve some kind of harmonious interaction so that they would be able to live in this place as well.

It is seen that he was very adept in that system in this type of task. He greatly enjoyed the so-called socialization aspect of learning how to deal with another species. He took this as a pleasant challenge and we see he enjoyed that colonization process.

We have here an existence which is not physical at all. It appears to be an inter-dimensional existence. There is a type of ectoplasmic energy which is less ectoplasm and more air, but it does have some form, but the form is wispy and able to change into a totally different form. We see that the being was again studying, but this time not in a colonization type of capacity, but rather observing the surface of a particular system. There were some beings from his inter-dimensional realms that wish to expand their civilization, but mostly they wish to expand their knowledge and understanding of what was present, what was out there both in outer space and inner space as well, so to speak. We see that the being is studying this one system and there is much traveling from system to system actually because it is seeking to understand communications between these various systems. The being comes with a great backlog of research and experience in working with different species.

The home system from which this being first differentiated is the Antares system; but in the interim between that differentiation and the other experiences there were other systems that this being lived on and in.

This client requested a reading for better spiritual understanding of his soul pattern. There was no particular present life trauma that needed to be addressed.

Chapter 3
A Clone who wants to Express her Individuality

We would like to start from the Source when this soul sparked off and began its evolvement, tracing the existences before it came to Earth.

We have here a scene where there is a darkness and as you go into this darkness there is a pulsation and a tone or a series of tones which come forth from this darkness. The pulsation is one of a certain kind of light. It is another dimension which the Earth beings are not familiar with. It is perhaps in another galactic system so we will try to describe this picture. We've gone through the darkness and there is this pulsating light. It is like two walls moving together sort of, but they don't quite meet; they bypass or interpenetrate each other. This light seems to be expanding and pulsating. It is pushing through the darkness. Perhaps this is the birth of this particular soul in this dimension that we are viewing because it is formless. There is an explosion as this light penetrates the darkness. This is like a sun almost, but not quite as large or quite as bright, and there is an explosion of sorts then a further light comes out from within this original light.

Now we see a place. It must be a planet. There appear to be life forms as we see it here. There is vegetation, but it is different from Earth type vegetation. There is a strange light source which is not like our sun around the Earth here. It has almost a silvery, bluish tinge to it. These large plant forms reach up towards this light source and that is what they feed off of. They are not rooted in a physical earth; they are rather almost floating on the surface of this sphere. The only similarity that we can describe is your Venus Fly Traps. Some of these look somewhat similar to those plant forms.

7

It is seen that there are some beings on the surface of this planet that are of a different substance than the plant life. Actually they seem to have more density than the plant life itself, and maybe because the molecular arrangement is more ordered and compacted, so they have a somewhat humanoid form. There are some variations to the structures- in fact; they prefer to move on all fours more than upright fashion. But this is not a density like the Earth's, so there is much more freedom of movement. They seem to be concerned with the surface of this planet so that's why they choose to move on all fours so they can better observe what is going on with the gases and the surfaces here.

Is this another galaxy?

Yes. So this cycle that we are viewing (we do not call it a lifetime). There are several beings that are almost like clones. This soul chooses to come into that civilization. The soul started in a what you would term structured and almost orderly fashion because this civilization that it first came into had a very structured and orderly systematic structure, like the beings were bred for a specific function, although the manner of reproduction was quite different and the density was not as great as that of the Earth plane at that time. So these beings that were on the surface here were made for the purpose of examining and taking data and so forth from various systems. Actually, this being put a rather small part of its soul into that form in order to learn about structure of a certain kind.

Then in the next cycle we see a being who appears to be very humanoid, whether there were others in between is not certain, but it appears that this being is on some type of mountain top, and again it does not appear to be solid but more of a light body. This time the being has less density than the planetary sphere and is again obviously watching and observing something. It appears that these beings were generated by the other beings and were reproduced. They were not your typical clones - they had the capacity of free thought. It is seen that this being that chose to come into that system at that time rebelled. In other words it did not wish to continue in that function, and there was a lot of dissension that was generated as a result of this. It was seen that the being would be better off if it went elsewhere so it chose to take on a different form or different evolutionary strain. The beings had free will, but there was a very orderly structured arrangement and most of the beings were satisfied with this arrangement. This being, however, was not satisfied and it developed a capacity of dissatisfaction because it was looking for more. It felt there was more and it developed a tremendous sense of self that it wished to explore and further develop.

The next scene is where this Light being is in another sphere. This sense of self is a two-fold thing because it has goaded it on and has kept it going and kept it experiencing. But on the other hand it has produced a certain sense of isolation from both humanity at large, which is shown later on down the line, but in another sense there is a certain closure within the mind of this being wherein it only allows so much. This is not to say that it is narrow-minded but it has some very definite thoughts and perhaps even feelings about certain matters and how things should function. This is one of the reasons that it chose not go into this very orderly and somewhat structured system, and it has carried that over.

Next we see the Light body looking at this planet and it has an unusual sense of sadness. Part of the sadness seems to stem from the fact that in the consciousness from that other cycle the being felt a sense of rejection because there was this warring tendency already within the being of wanting to evolve on the one hand and there was this other input that it was not okay for that being to exercise its individuality to the degree that it wished, even though the capacity was there and the potential was there, and that system allowed for those potentials. But the way the system functioned they just simply made those beings go elsewhere. So there was also this feeling of rejection which started very early on in this soul's history. It is seen that even to this day the soul yet carries that sense that it feels it will be rejected.

There are continued long descriptions of various existences off-Earth. I am skipping much of the reading to go to Athor's concluding remarks about this client's soul.

The soul has chosen to experience the Earth density in order for it to learn how to re-manifest the Light. By this we mean to obtain a sufficient degree of soul consciousness while in this density to transmute and bring forth the Light through all these levels. It has this whole string of existences behind it in other spheres and in other energy forms. It was always looking for more, and it always wanted to learn more. But its particular path and progress has been to come more and more into density in an almost sequential manner rather than jumping around here and there and having all these different experiences as different life forms. In between the existences there have been Light body experiences on other spheres and other planes but it was only when it came in through the Earth sphere that it developed the capacity to expand itself in the Light body. So this is a most unique experience and experiment on the soul's part. It wishes to embody the Light form through the physical into the planetary sphere through a body. It wishes to achieve full consciousness so it will never again miss out. There is a feeling within this being that it has missed out on something somewhere. It wants to get rid of that feeling because it has spent eons going more and more, further and further into density in order to experience the gamut of how the consciousness evolves through these forms and through this density. It has had a real thirst and a thrust and desire to experience this. The soul is ready for another evolutionary step. In this lifetime it will complete the cycles, then the Light body will move on. In this cycle the soul wishes to ground the Light and to expand the Light and to understand ...to become consciously aware of all the cycles previously that have led to this time now. The soul is ready to move on, basically, and to expand into other realms and other dimensions which will be less physical. This being's Light body has reached a point where now in this life cycle it can achieve that awareness of itself - that awareness of the soul Light, the soul essence, as an entity within itself. From then it will move on.

The reading ended with a visualization to assist the client in achieving its goal for this lifetime. This client was in the Army. Her exposure to metaphysics was fairly recent. It seems that she apparently subconsciously chose to join the Army because it had structure, but as in the very early existence, she has become discontented, wanting to develop her own individual personality. Her presenting issue was "What should I do with the rest of my life?" Athor did not know my client was in the Army until the end of the reading when she asked, "What kind of work do you do?" Her comment to my client was "Well, you can't get much more structured than that!"

Chapter 4
An Aspect of a Future Self
Greater Brain Expansion

This client is a brilliant scientist. He was wondering what happened to him when he was ten years old and in the hospital. When he came home he suddenly found he was able to work highly advanced mathematical problems. Earlier he was simply a very average student with no particular ability in math.

When the being first came in for this session, there was a noticeable energy which is not commonly found in most beings. The being has a most perceptive capacity and quality within the auric field. We are trying to see in the auric field. (Long pause) There are two balls of light here. This does not appear to be entirely like the one stepping out and the other one stepping in (as in cases of Walk-Ins). It's not simply a higher aspect of the being, but like a future cycle of that soul. This is what would be termed an overshadowing of another Light force here, but it is not replacing your soul (*My client had thought he might be a Walk-In*). It is simply in very close proximity to your soul, to your Light body. It would appear that it is there to aid and assist. It is there for your benefit and your growth. This does not appear to be a soul braiding. (*Athor is trying to decide just what kind of experiment this is since we had never done a reading before for someone with this particular pattern*).

(*Long pause*) It is another dimensional self, you might say, from a future time which has come forth more or less overshadowing this being, kind of watching over it, but also quickening its growth and development. There seems to be a need to pull this particular being up into a certain level and to get on with whatever it is. There seems to be a need to quicken the normal evolutionary process in this particular case.

So to clarify, this would be a higher essence of his soul that would be from a possible future life.

Let's now go to his question about his purpose for this lifetime.

It would appear that this being had many off-Earth existences in what you term your Pleiadian system. It was at this time that the being was being readied for a transference. The being is being prepared and is still in the preparatory stages for this to occur. Because of his connection with the Pleiadian system the being is being monitored but not in the normal fashion such as those who have monitors in the head, and implants. This is another dimensional type of activity that is occurring. This is all occurring on the inner realms on other levels. All I am hearing is they are saying, "We are preparing this being for a quantum leap" as the cellular mechanism is undergoing rapid changes." It's like the whole body structure is being in a sense elongated. It's like he is being prepared to be a vessel, and the vessel has to be sufficiently clear and strong to be able to contain the energy which wishes to come forth into this vessel. We have an image of a plasma body. This is very dense but not as dense as the physical and it is not quite etheric. It is a mixture between etheric and water. We have this image of a protoplasm type of being that will merge into this physical vehicle when the transference is complete. Again, this is not so much another being as a future or more advanced form of this particular being. It is already living in another dimensional frequency and it wishes to join you to bring the totality of its essence to bear fruit. It's like an experiment in a way, but we do not see it as a negative experiment, but it wishes to join and it wishes to expand, etc.

This protoplasmic being wishes to come forth first through a computer like device because that is like the beginning stages of connecting more fully and consciously into the consciousness of this being. It is more in terms of mathematical coordinates and energy fields rather than words. Through the computer it will bring it through into this dimension. As the link becomes stronger and stronger, and as the fusion begins to take hold, the being will undergo a mental and physical transformation of sorts which if it allows it to occur will be quite pleasant. If there is resistance then it can be somewhat unpleasant. It is suggested that the being, knowing that it is not of a negative nature, allows this to occur without any undo restrictions or obstructions.

Until this fusion has been effected, there is very little that we can say about what this advanced being would wish to do because at that time you will have an access to so many parts of yourself which are now somewhat dormant. The average human being uses less than 5% of its brain capacity. Many beings from other galactic systems utilize much more of this capacity. So this aspect of yourself coming from the future is like one of the "New Beings" here on Earth.

It is seen that there was a cycle wherein there was some scientific research. It was at this time that the being first gained a conscious knowledge or interest in these types of potentialities, shall we say. The being was involved at the time in something to do with astronomy, but it had to do with physics of some type as well. The being was interested in some of the material which Tesla had come forth with and indeed it is seen that the being himself had many of the similar capacities which the being Tesla had, but much was still quite blocked. It is seen that these memories are yet very much in the psyche, in the consciousness and that the information which was acquired then is going to be in good stead. It will be very valuable to this being because once this opens up it is like a whole network opens up inside the brain and the cellular memories will become almost like a prototype of a brain of future civilizations.

I had wanted very much to do a follow up on this client to see how this scenario unfolded, but unfortunately not long after his Athor reading he sold his home in California and accepted a new position with a company located in Colorado. The move out of state was a huge opportunity for him but unfortunately I lost touch with him so am not sure how this "experiment" developed.

Chapter 5
A Very Different Off-Earth Experience

What is the origin of this soul?

It appears that this soul originated in a realm which is not of the physical plane. It chose to remain in what you would term a disembodied state before coming to the Earth plane. This was somewhere between the astral and causal planes. It is not a plane of unbounded energies as would be found in electrical planes and frequencies of that sort. These energies are bounded in molecular aggregates which appear almost amorphous. They do have some type of shape, but they are amorphous to the normal human understanding as each one has such a peculiar shape that you would almost say it is amorphous. The being has an innate understanding of the composition of certain textures and textural qualities, an innate comprehension of molecular bonding and aggregates. There were many, many cycles evolving from that plane or that point. She went through planes and dimensions wherein there was just a flatness. These were not three dimensional aspects but linear type of planes. The being did not just simply leave the logos and plop into the human dimension. It evolved from various energetic frequencies, and it is seen that it did choose the Earth plane experience as it came through these other planes and dimensions. It did not first go into a certain form in another galaxy or planet such as you know a form. These were very different structures that this being chose to live in for experience. It is most difficult to try to explain and understand the vibrational quality of what we are seeing. This is really the best that we can do in transmitting this information.

Why did she choose to come to Earth?

Because it had seen that in the various processes of its cycles and evolutionary phases between and betwixt the different planes and dimensions and energies, it began to see like a chain of succession. It began to see in its eyes, in a sense, a beginning, and leading to some type of end although it was not aware of the end. It used some of the linear focus that it had acquired and wished to move along an evolutionary, A,B,C,D, etc. The being saw that the building blocks that it had experienced in former cycles all gradually built one upon the other. Having had this capacity and innate knowingness when it was this molecular aggregate, it then chose to build further and take all these steps and bring together a form which incorporated in many ways all the others that it had experienced. It wished to see the synthesis of all these prior cycles. It simply brought them all together, and wished to see it put together in perhaps a different type of form, a form that had certain limitations, shall we say, because the being had not experienced this before. All these other forms did not have the limitations and the structure that the physical form has.

What is the purpose of human life?

That is entirely dependent upon the view from which one views that question. There is no one set answer per se. This individual has had certain experiences along with other so called evolutionary strains which have nothing to do with the Earth plane per se, and has incorporated on an inner level all this knowledge and these capacities, and this being wishes to see both what the limits of this human form and human vessel and incarnation are, as well as the full range of capacities. It wished to experience the combination of qualities and allow the mental capacities a full rein of ability to expand through the human form. It had not had that experience until it entered the human form. This soul simply saw it as a further step in its particular evolutionary cycles. The human condition taken as a whole is to be seen simply as a learning process and a great and divine playground, in a sense, although many of you do not choose to view it as a playground, for many of you chose to gather experiences which would produce what you would term suffering, pain and deprivation. However, depending upon the nature of the consciousness, the Earth plane is a tremendous playground. It is a place wherein all the different faculties, capacities and abilities from various and sundry realms can be brought together and experienced in as a cohesive manner as possible. This is because on the human plane you have the beginning capacity of Divine will channeled through a physicalized form. This is one of the few places in your universe wherein this is possible. There are others wherein there is a semi-physical and semi-solid type of existence. There are many others; but the Earth plane itself has a number of differences. One of them is that the Divine will is coupled both in and through the physical vehicle. There is a distinct connection between the higher qualities of Divine will coming through the chakras and into the physical plane dimension. In less physicalized beings and forms there is a very different energy connective mechanism; your chakra system here is peculiar to the Earth plane variety of vessels.

This client's main issue was marital problems which were addressed in an earlier part of the reading. She traveled quite a distance to get a reading and attend my monthly group meetings (OMRA). She seemingly is on the path to becoming a strong Light worker.

19

Chapter 6
A Desire for Power

Some concerned grandparents requested a reading for their five year old grandson. Their daughter was finding it increasingly difficult to control the boy. The root of his control issue was found in a past off-Earth life with his present Earth mother.

We see a cycle wherein there is a female form sitting upon a small hill in the countryside and there is a small group of younger beings sitting at the feet of this one. She is teaching them the ways of nature and how to forage for certain plants and minerals and things of that sort. So the children go out and each one brings out a particular stone, a crystal formation, and they put them all in a circular formation at the feet of this woman. Then she goes over and lays her hand over these stones. There seems to be some sparks, tremendous flashes of light coming, going forth between the body of this being and the stones. It seems that she is teaching them to tame the powers of these stones so that they will be ready to be worked with for the purposes that they have chosen.

This one young boy who seems to be the present child is standing there apart from the group and he is quite fascinated. But there is some other quality here. He wishes to understand this process, but not for the purpose of working for the whole with all the others and bringing harmony, not for that purpose. He is intrigued by the power aspect, and this woman, he observes, is capable of seeing the auric lights and energy frequencies visually. He also sees the frequency and the light and what is charging what. He observes it minutely and determines that he will utilize it for his own purposes.

After everyone has left, he goes over to this group of rocks and crystals, and he puts his hands over them as she has done, and he recharges them with his raw essence. Whereas the woman has gently civilized the power of these crystals he has returned the raw power to them. He takes several of them, the ones that seem to have taken most of that recharge back, and he takes those away from the group of other crystals. He takes them into a hillside and hides them there. Then he goes out and searches for some others to put there.

Now out of all these young people there, he was the only one whose vision was adequately developed at that time to see the light rays that came forth. The woman could see all the light rays and the energetic frequencies and thus she was able to tame the power of these crystals. He tried desperately to find similar ones that would sort of get her off track, so to speak. There was a process where they had to remain there for a certain period of time after this was done, and so they remained there since she had done her thing with them. She did not return. Someone else came who did not have the vision that she did to see that these were not the same rocks, that the energies were very different, etc. So he just gathered them up and took them to do whatever, never noticing or realizing that there were some missing.

In the meantime this child who was the approximate age of 10 went into where he had hidden the rocks that he took and began working with them individually – exchanging energy, drawing forth energy, putting in energy, sucking energy out and trying all sorts of permutations with the intent of power. A great deal of energy was generated from this group of rocks which he had hidden. The energy that radiated forth was seen coming forth from the hillside, from beneath the ground. The light and the rays came forth and were observed by a few individuals who had their sight fully developed. They became very curious because this was not part of the prearranged plan. In the meantime this young man had set up a force field with the aid and assistance of certain energies which would bar any entrance but his own into the hillside towards this treasured group of crystals.

As these individuals approached, they were repelled by this force field and they had to call a meeting. The woman came forth and they asked her to utilize her abilities which were of a different, gentler frequency, but none the less quite powerful, as there was this spiritual connection. They asked her to go to the hillside to see what she could do. As she approached the mountain, the child came forth and told her to stop. He would not permit her physical access into this hillside. A great discussion ensued. Finally she left with some sorrow because she saw that she could not forcibly take hold and redo this entire energetic process and pattern. She concluded that he had to do his own thing and so she had to leave him to fulfill whatever he was doing there with his energies. This created a disharmony in that community and thus he was more or less ostracized and isolated, not with any vengeance, but rather out of necessity since he did not wish to associate with the others anymore.

He moved on and went to another town and started trying to work on those people and did his little power trips. There was a great sadness in this woman. She hoped and fervently prayed that through love and through compassion she could one day save this being and help his soul manifest its spiritual self – to bring about an integration of the power and the spiritual. This is the mother of this child in this lifetime.

After receiving the reading, the grandmother wrote:

We have finally listened to the tape, and the reading for our grandson. It amazed us, yet didn't surprise us, for we had sensed the strength - the self-willed strength of the child, and knew that he needed very careful guidance, firm discipline and the learning of self-discipline. His mother has lavished patience and love upon him, but sometimes has lacked in firmness.

Can you give some idea about the age of this soul?

This soul is in terms of Earth lives fairly young. However, it is indicated that this being has had numerous incarnations upon other planes and spheres, and thus the manner of incarnation in this cycle is one of great curiosity, and one of studying and learning about interactions of cause and effect. The soul has been in a differentiated form for many, many eons of time. However, it is relatively new to the Earth's sphere. In terms of Earth lives, this particular being has had a relatively few number of incarnations.

I am getting a tremendous headache. *(The headache apparently was caused by the energy of this child's attachment).* There is an energy here looking in upon this reading which is intrusive. This energy is rather dark, but a persuasive energy and mettlesome type of energy. It seems to be connected to this child.

Does this child have an attachment?

An attachment, yes, and this attachment is not human. This child has beings watching over it that have a particular interest in its development. It is like they are using this child as a laboratory to study things for themselves. This energy, through its connections with this young child, is gaining information and knowledge that it is learning from him. Yet it is seen that this almost symbiotic connection is not what you would term beneficial to the child. It is seen that this child has what you would term almost an infinite opening in the area of the solar plexus at this time and it is through this chakra connection that this energy has made contact and is in essence a symbiotic relationship in the auric field of this child. Thus we have here a case wherein the child is not autonomous in its own auric space. This is an implantation carried over from a former cycle in which the being dealt with many and varied energies, dealing with cause and effect. The child was responsible for generating many causes on a large scale, many of which were not beneficial to others or in harmony. It is like an insatiable energy that is totally divorced from the emotional aspect. It is not the child itself, but is an energy which is in the field of this young child. It seeks to devour everything. It has an insatiable appetite for knowledge, in particular, on how to create and cause certain things to occur and how to move events and people. This implant occurred wherein the auric field was weakened and opened to this influence.

The child needs structure beginning with teaching him meditative techniques at an early age as a manner of discipline, a type of discipline that will allow it to feel its own life force, to feel its own energy and begin to center within. He needs to be taught not something etheric and philosophical and way out, but a grounding through the physical and higher centers.

Athor continues to give much detail on how to achieve this, which I am eliminating, because each individual soul would need a different plan, depending on the past life patterns, etc. The grandparents felt the reading was very helpful, although the mother of the child is a traditional Christian and does not believe in reincarnation, so they will feed information to her gradually in order to help this boy grow up to be a caring adult.

Chapter 7
Birth of a Soul and a Difficult Relationship

This client had asked for a Source Reading, but her underlying problem was her relationship with a man much younger than my client. We begin with the Source Reading which is rather bizarre, then ends with an explanation of the soul relationship between my client and her boyfriend. She knows it is not a healthy relationship and she has tried to break it off a number of times, but somehow they always come back together. This is an example of how strong off-Earth ties can be. When one partner is much younger than the other, and the relationship is not suitable for this lifetime, it usually goes back to off-Earth lives.

I see something similar to a cell mitosis where the nucleus begins to divide and there are two cell-like structures. One goes on; it appears it is pulled in what would be termed an upward direction and the other one remains. The one remaining begins to vibrate. It seems to birth itself on some unusual level. It is as Light, but nothing like seen here on planet Earth. There are certain tones or frequencies that are given off. It appears that around this image is a laboratory. There are beings watching this energy source. These beings are very tall and somewhat angular in appearance, apparently scientists of some kind. They are viewing this mitosis, or whatever you call it. It is still in the very early, most primitive stages while this is being viewed. One of them goes into some vials and it is seen that a certain magnetic field, if applied to this energy source, creates a tremendous pressure on it, much akin to the pressure that is exerted on a piece of coal over millions of years to turn it into a diamond. This pressure is applied to this energy source which responds by exerting a pressure of its own. In the process of that the two fuse or come together. A being emerges from within this cell-like structure. Now there is a being that is of a different substance than these others that are doing this experiment. This being appears to be a little less dense than these other beings. It is shaped in a humanoid fashion, but its head is more rounded; all the features are more rounded, although it is fairly tall. This being begins to float or flit about this laboratory. It is most intrigued and curious as to all these gadgets and all these different things, etc. It comes before one of these beings and enters this being, as it is of a less dense substance. In so doing there is a tremendous explosion of energy within, and there is an image of denser energies being hurtled outward and away. The other beings are experiencing this explosion type thing, and so they are running for cover. They pull some buttons and a force field, a shield, is put up between them and the one the being has entered.

As a result of this fusion, there is yet another being formed. There is a new creation being born. This is a being that is composed of finer matter than the former being. This is quite a metamorphosis. The other beings are curious. There is a little fear, but it seems as though this is all to be taken in stride. They didn't quite know the extent of what would occur. They were prepared on some level for this type of eventuality. And so they lower the force field; they dissipate it. They go towards this new being, and they communicate. There seems to be a friendly feeling. They are not afraid. There is a feeling on some level that this has been a successful experiment. And so they became acquainted and fill this new being in on a lot of details. (*Where did they get this energy?*) It is almost like they cloned it from various energies or frequencies that they had gathered. Somehow with the apparatus they were able to merge certain energies into a very unique combination you might say. This being appears to be you (*my client*). This was one of your first early introductions where your soul wished to experience and experiment with different life forms and with the permutations and changes that can occur with different species or form. So the soul sought to live in or inhabit this particular nucleus that they had in the laboratory.

Can you identify where this laboratory was?

It was in the Andromeda system. After that the being became somewhat of a celebrity. It gained quite a deal of status because it was a most successful experiment. There was much studying. The experimenters constantly asked it questions, and there would be tests and different things to find out every little detail of how this process worked. This had only been done one time, and though the scientists had a record of what had been done, they needed to get a greater understanding. The being was like a hybrid in a sense, and was looked upon with great favor. The being became a leader in this particular area and spent a very, very long time in that capacity, becoming almost as though one of the elders of that race or that particular group of beings, if you will. It had the position of an elder or wise being that they turned to for advice.

Next I have an image of a light streaking across the cosmos. It appears to be almost like a fireball. It comes forth in a sphere. It seems like a fireball. The being drops into another sphere. It pulsates and adds to this sphere when it pulsates, and at the same time it takes in some of the substances of that sphere. There is an exchange, and it is learning in that state something about these elements, though not in any humanly conscious terminology. It is not humanoid at all. It is seen that it dives down into a sea of this swelling, etheric lava would be the closest word. When it does so it becomes much more densified. It is almost like it becomes part of that substance. We are not sure if this is the beginning stages of the creation of a planet or what, but it is almost frozen there. This is very difficult to describe. It is not trapped. It has just become part of this sea, this etheric, swelling, gaseous substance. Then we see that it has changed color, but is still in somewhat the shape of a ball. When it leaves that dimension, it also leaves that substance behind. It is similar to the human form when the physical body dies. The light goes on and this is what we are viewing here. It has again gone into this ball of light.

I have a scene where there are a lot of flying ships and it seems like the sky is dotted with them. They are taking off and landing, taking off and landing. There are two individuals on this field looking in the sky at these flying saucers or whatever, and they are discussing the universe and how well they are doing. It would seem that both of them know one of the beings in one of the crafts in the sky. Then they go into a structure that leads underground. It is almost like an elevator. They are taken underground where there is a whole base. It is quite large and extremely well lit from strange light sources. They are going over to a large council type place. From this place they can view other parts of the galaxy. It seems that this is where they are connected. Through this council they are connected to the crafts. And through this connection they can view what the crafts are viewing wherever they are.

They have been talking about the craft that had been on a maneuver somewhere. As they are watching on the monitor, they see the craft and they see that it suddenly explodes. Both of these beings are watching and there is a tremendous feeling of horror that overcomes them because there is one of their loved ones in that craft. It would almost appear as if they are man and wife, although they do not appear to be male and female, but similar in appearance. However, the vibratory frequency is one of male. Neither of them can continue watching. We see that one is putting an arm around the other one and they leave the council and someone else takes over.

They go back out and again are viewing the sky and the crafts, but there is much longing and sorrow. It is a big mixture of feelings and emotions. It is seen that one of these beings finally collapses on the surface, and there appears to be sad emotions. The other one is walking away. Because the other one cannot deal with what has occurred, and the other is seen walking away because it has enough of its own feelings and cannot help this other one at this time. As it walks away, it is seen that one craft sends a beam down and seriously injures this being that was walking away. Apparently the person in the craft was trying to aim, and they didn't aim properly and pushed the wrong button. They weren't supposed to use this ray, but it was an accident. The form of this being was seriously damaged and seriously injured. It is seen the spinal area was almost completely exposed. The being was lingering with some life force left. The other one rushed over because it knew it had walked away. It rushed over and found him in bad shape. You tried to rescue him but he was beyond help and it was beyond hope at that point that the being's life force expired. This being *(my client)* was the one who tried to help and the being who died was her present boyfriend.

How many existences have they had together?

Maybe six? The theme has always been one of loss.

What needs to be done to complete that relationship in this lifetime?

It is seen that the other being does not have the consciousness yet to comprehend or understand these past cycles. Therefore, there cannot be a conscious effort on both parts to come together to resolve these issues. However, it is indicated that the lady here today does have the capacity to heal this within herself, to come into a full understanding that these kinds of cycles have been repeated many times in one form or another, and that she, by the mere fact of becoming conscious of this can thus change this so-called scenario and bring about a feeling so that both parties may be released. There should be fewer attempts at trying to pull him in and more of an effort put into healing him. Send a loving light and a loving energy which will release this being from this cycle and these binds. This is not to say, release the physical body, but certainly from these cycles. It would be wise to undergo some type of program which would allow her to release these emotions and the hurt, the pain, the yearning and longing – all of these things which are yet deep within her. It can be done by her, but is helpful to be done in the presence of an understanding individual so that she can be guided through some of these feelings and experiences.

My client did eventually leave this mate and moved on with her life. She is a highly spiritual person who will always love this man at a soul level, but with the knowledge of their past life cycles she was able to understand the emotions that brought them together again. He had simply not matured enough in this lifetime for them to be suitable mates this time around.

Chapter 8
A Soul Braid

This client's eighteen year old son had previously been identified as a soul braid in progress. His mother later requested a reading for herself. We wish to trace the origins of this soul.

We see a ball of light streaking across the cosmos. It comes down upon a plane and splits into many different forms like a waterfall, a shower of light. The showers of light take on a rather strange form. They all seem to be connected to this main source, but they're all like squiggly little creatures or something, but they are still Light forms. They are not physical or of any great density. It's something like a central unit which has all these things attached to it. They are on like a bungee cord and they can stretch and go out so far, but then they have to come back. It seems that this was one of the first attempts to become differentiated, but yet there was still the desire to remain a whole unit. But the whole unit of Light was not ready to make such a giant leap, you might say; it differentiated in very small stages. It came as the Light and then that Light didn't quite separate but came into these many different parts which were still connected. It seems that it was a creature of Light but nothing known to human form.

Next we see a form that is like a golden octopus with many tentacles, and then there is still the main section. The being at that time was gaining experience; the Light body was gaining experience in the expansive and contractive qualities. It wished to experience that and this was one of the first experiences in that sphere.

Was this in our galaxy or a different galaxy where this was taking place?

This was in this galactic system, but in some other planes and dimensions. We are still viewing this being like an octopus, but this light is not dense or physical. One of these tentacles seems to have disengaged and is shooting out from this place; there is a very large magnetic field that follows this appendage, this streak of light and the magnetic field engulfs the tentacle. It streaks away but it can only go so far. It seems to go a great distance, but this magnetic field pulls it back. It is seen that the Light body spent quite a time in this experience because it is seen that this form of Light becomes more structured. It becomes somewhat denser in form, in frequency. It is still Light, but it has achieved a greater density, and it appears to be something like a gigantic spider in shape. This form gives birth, it is seen, to many other forms of Light. It is as though these appendages of Light somehow have the capacity to reproduce themselves and so we see many small forms that have been created. There is this gigantic figure of a spider-like Light that hovers over them. This was the beginning of the sensation of nurturing and almost a parental type of quality. It is interesting because the image of that Light form in its spider-like form hovering over all these other small spiders seem to be symbolic; but also there is a very deep, deep memory within the psyche of this individual - that protective, nurturing, hovering quality has gained some deep roots. It is like a mother hen watching over the brood type of thing. It seems that this Light being did populate a great part of this plane that we are viewing. It took on the role of the mother hen more perhaps then the role of a Creator as there was much more of a protective nurturing, rather than the dominate tendency *(My client has ten children in this lifetime).*

We still see the same plane. The being acquired the capacities for what you would term some of the more human type emotional characteristics; the sense of longing for love and protective nurturing. All of these types of things develop with this being on this plane, and it is seen that the being created all these various Light forms on that plane, therefore it felt very protective of them.

What dimension are you seeing?

We hear the fifth. It is seen that the being spent a great deal of time *(an Earth term)* there watching over and guiding the development of these Light forms. Since it had created them, it became a teacher and was very much interested in passing on its knowledge and wisdom. Although this was totally different from the human realm, many of the sensations of emotion were present there, although there were no physical capacities for any of this type of response.

Now there is an opening that was created into this dimension and a new energy source intruded itself. In symbolic representation it was almost like a bolt of lightning which came and split this plane and put a wedge of energy into this plane. As a result of this, the plane became more crystalized; it froze the energies. It slowed down the vibratory frequencies and everything slowed considerably so that the beings that were on this plane became more frozen in their electro-magnetic activities so they acquire a denser, slower rate as a result of this. It forced the being into a different level of existence, you might say. We see a gap between the consciousness of that level which had been accustomed to the nurturing, and all that. Then suddenly there was this further densification; and it is seen that there is an imbalance in the outer fields of this being due to the fact that this was like a shock on those inner levels. This came as a great shock, and as a consequence there is an imbalance. We have here the capacity and the recognition of the higher realms and the higher frequencies. From there to a denser level is like a quantum leap which does not expand the being, but simply seems to imprison it. And so there is a gap, a lack of access of this information; the higher frequencies cannot come through. It's like the being went into shock and froze. It became crystalized in a certain form which was not yet physical, but very dense compared to its former existence and level. We find that the consciousness itself almost seems to have frozen in this crystalline structure that's similar to a rock, but is not physical. It is seen that a being comes. This was like an intrusion of another energy from another dimensional frequency. And this other energy did not just happen. It was brought about by beings from another frequency. They were experimenting, if you will. It is seen that there is this sort of rock-like looking mass where the being had become crystalized, and we see some light and energies which are being directed at this mass. It is seen that the form of this mass where it had become crystalized began to separate and almost melt in a sense from the original Light body, then the energy is released. It becomes one with a certain element which is again not physical, but it is a mixture between a gaseous and a dewy state. It is seen that it takes this on to experience this sensation and to learn about this element; for it is seen that it had need of it for a future time.

There follows a long discourse of various other experiments with energies. Athor finally finds this soul in a more physical incarnation.

The soul did not wish to become a consciousness that was individualized. Apparently it was enjoying its "scientific" experiments and was reluctant to incarnate on a planet. We have here a civilization that was your planet Pluto. There also seems to have been some communicating with Mars. These beings we are viewing have a much greater density than has heretofore been seen in this soul's evolution. These beings do not appear to have any particular spiritual inclinations. They are very one pointed and scientifically inclined. It's almost like the being made a huge jump from that level of being somewhat impersonal to the opposite extreme to where it was very grounded in this civilization. However, this civilization was unaware of any other frequencies or vibrations other than their pursuits from their levels of research. They were not aware of anything less dense than they themselves. This is most difficult to get because it appears this is a traumatic cycle. Some of beings are discussing something dealing with the flying craft. It is like the craft was set to certain specifications and these two that are viewing have something else in mind. And so they are changing the setting of this particular craft, and this setting is designed to kill whoever it is that will be flying in it because it will not respond to the normal maneuvers. It is seen that it is this being here who is the one that is going in this craft and another being goes with her. It appears to be from that time one of her children was in that cycle. It is a younger person but appears to be close to adult size. We see the being is in the craft and is checking the dials and instruments and it notices a peculiarity in one of the instrument panels. There is a light given off which will not go out. It checks it and double checks it. All of the beings observing this are asked to look into this and to make certain before takeoff to be sure everything is all right. However, they are unable to program this out and the light does not change. They became aware that this could be a fatal malfunction and they are forced to make a choice because it appears that the mission that they are going on is very important for some reason. Everybody else is already taking off, and they are part of a group. And so, the leader, who happens to be the being here, has to make a decision. It makes the decision to go ahead, and as a result of this there is a tremendous guilt that came about within this psyche's soul history. It is seen that as a result of this decision, the craft exploded and all the other beings that were there as well were obliterated from their form.

I need some clarification. The child went with her on the craft, but there were other members of the crew on board as well.

Yes. It is seen that there were others there also.

All right, what was the motivation of the beings that set this up to make the craft explode?

It is seen that they did not wish this one to advance beyond a certain point. It was not so much this one as the child. Knowing that the child would be on the craft as well, it was really the child that was the target. Since this being was the one heading and piloting the craft, this was a very underhanded operation. It was a psychological ploy because they knew that when she checked the instruments, she would recognize that something was not the same. They wanted to kill the child and they realized that even though she became aware that something was not all right, the fact that the dedication to the mission and the importance of what was to be done would probably be the overriding factor, and the being would ignore the malfunctioning light and continue on the mission. The explosion of the craft created a great spiritual shock for the being.

There follows much discussion of how to release the negative energy from that experience. This leads into the discovery that there is another presence in the being that is distinctly different from the other. Are there two consciousnesses?

It would appear to be so.

Is this being a soul braid in this lifetime?

I hear yes.

Could you give an approximate time period when it happened?

Somewhere between age 15 to 22. It is seen that from the spinal cord at the top there is like this fountain, but it goes only two directions, and the energy is mixing in the spinal column of the two energies.

Where is this other soul from?

I hear Alpha Centauri.

What is the purpose of this soul braid?

This is really strange, because these energies are very powerful and very magnetic. It doesn't wish to reveal very much of anything. Well, it is saying that we have come here to both observe and finalize. It is like putting the final touches on something, and that is very strange.

Can you give the approximate number of incarnations this being has had on Earth.

Approximately 120.

She's been around for a long time. Has the Alpha Centauri being been on Earth before?

I hear yes.

When did that incarnate? See if you can find out about that. Was it a body that was a single soul, or did it go into a body that was also a soul braid?

This goes back to a lifetime as a youth in Greece.

So maybe there was a soul braiding of the being's soul and this being from Alpha Centauri back in the early Greek times. How many times have these two souls been braided together?

Three.

Athor had determined that one of this client's sons is in the process of becoming a soul braid.

Will any more of this being's children become soul braids? (Athor asks for the children to be named one by one.

Athor then identifies three of the children as possible soul braids. I then ask if the child that was killed in the explosion of the craft was one of her children in this lifetime. She names her two year old as the child from the Pluto existence.)

Can you give a name to this being that has joined with Rebecca (not real name)?

It is Silviatar. It is well to remember that the nurturing qualities with which you became so familiar eons ago have indeed served you well in past cycles. However, it is also suggested that you become aware of the other parts of you, the more assertive and perhaps more dominant part of your being. It is this part which is trying to balance itself together with the energies of Silviatar. This other being seeks to learn, and there can be a great exchange between the two parts of yourself essentially. It is seen that not only are you here to bring forth certain qualities in these children, but you also are here to help this being expand and learn so that you can benefit from its energies within yourself and it can benefit from yours. It seems to have come in because you have had so many cycles of the feminine qualities. These energies are very strong in your soul's light.

In all the cycles in the earlier times you did not develop a very strong individualized expression in terms of mental dominance type of capacity. This soul braid is almost the opposite end of the scale because it has none of these qualities which you have been so experienced in. The energies we see are twined in the spinal cord to bring these two qualities together into a harmonious whole. If you pay attention to it, you will be more conscious and develop in these areas.

I later heard that my client had gotten a divorce. She had stated that he was an abusive husband, and with ten children she had felt trapped. However, after this reading she seemed to finally be asserting herself. She moved from the area and the last I heard from her she was trying to figure out what she wanted to do with her life.

I have discovered that part of this reading is in Book One, but this is much longer including more information than the condensed form for my newsletter.

Chapter 9
An Implant

David came for a reading because he was convinced that he had an alien implant. He had a list of unusual questions, but we are going to start from the evolvement of the soul from the Source. Athor, as usual, asks for the complete name.

We see an image of what you would term a star that has a tremendous light radiating forth from it. It would appear from some vantage points to be almost like a sun because of the incredible amount of light that seems to emanate from it, but is much smaller in size. It is seen that there are beings upon this star, within this star system that are not in physical forms such as is on the Earth plane. The density is much less. And these beings come from between fifth and sixth densities. There is a great loving fluidic motion with these beings. They are entirely propelled by thought. The beings appear to be somewhat similar in appearance to what was shown in the movie "Cocoon", as they appear to be somewhat humanoid; however, there is not the physical density. The beings on this star system are very energetic and industrious. They have many dealings with many galactic systems it would appear. They are in a continual mode of both teaching and learning as they are ever seeking to grow. Being between fifth and sixth density, they have acquired a knowledge and wisdom far beyond what is commonly known upon the Earth plane at this time. Nonetheless, they are still in the growth process. It would appear that this being was on this star system somewhat recently.

Was this the original existence then on that star system?

There have been others but this seems to be the main thrust of the energy towards this system.

Can you identify the star system?

Betelgeuse in the Orion star system. These beings are involved in a number of colonization projects. There appears to be an energy that on Earth would be considered negative that is also part of this system. It is almost as though this system is split almost completely in half. One half is moving only in the Light and within the Light while the other half wishing to serve what you would term more the self with the small 's'. Occasionally there are beings from the dark side of the system that come upon this plane as well and intermingle, as they also have various interests, and theirs are a different orientation.

Which side is David (not real name) on?

This being is most definitely of the Light, but it is also seen that in the auric system at this moment there is a certain imbalance of the energies as there appears to be a darker side to the auric field and a lighter side which is so indicative of this star system, for the being's left side is a darker configuration of energy than is seen on the right.

Is that where you had an implantation?

Yes, that is where they implanted it. We had seen earlier that these darker beings of that system had had something to do with this connection in some way. Whether it was the original so called abduction that occurred in between or at some other time is not certain, but there has been an energy induction which is not of the Light. That is why you have this beeping and buzzing because it is not in harmony with your energy system.

Can you determine why the device was placed in his ear?

It is the intent of these particular beings to gain access to knowledge of the thoughts, patterns, and emotional reactions of what you term Homo Sapiens. They have much interest in learning of the genetic makeup and things of that sort, for they have their own ideas of what they would like to do. It is actually much easier to implant such a device so they would be able to monitor through the eyes, through the ears and through the body of beings that they wish to study. Now it is a darker energy which is seen as an intrusion, in the sense that the being has not consciously had full knowledge or recognition of the source of this particular implantation.

Let's go to some more specific questions. What is David's highest purpose for being here on Earth at this particular time?

This being is and has been in many ways a Light bearer. However, there has been an equally strong interest from the other so called polarity from his system, and consequently at this time it is seen that there is a difficulty because of this implantation device. It is emitting a frequency which is harmonious to the beings that implanted it, but is not harmonious to this being's system. As a result of this, not only is there a beeping, but there is the darkening of the auric field because it is not in harmony with this being's frequency. Part of what is going on is a longing on your soul's part that you are trying to be of assistance to the dark side of your system in order to help them evolve as well. That is why you have allowed this to occur. This may not be at a conscious level; but nonetheless, that is an element that we see here. It has been your soul's desire to be of assistance that you have allowed this to occur. It is not that you are seen as a victim, as such, because truly on the deepest level, none are.

Can this implant be removed, or is that something that David is just going to have to adapt to?

45

That is entirely up to the decision of the soul. If it wishes to be of assistance to its system, then it will choose to allow this to remain or perhaps make some adaptations to it, for with the clarity and the insight of these various chakra systems functioning, there is also the capability to either remove or change the frequency of this device. It is evident that the individual has the capacity to function through these various chakra systems and because of that has the ability to handle this himself, depending on his decision.

It is suggested that you take some time by yourself and raise your frequencies from the lowest chakra up to the highest and that you do this three times, going from the lowest to the highest, expanding both into the chakra and around into your auric bodies. At the completion of the third time of doing this, you should go within wherever you feel that you can sense or feel. You can ask to be shown a greater picture of how to get greater clarity of your system and your connection with that system. This will bring this into fuller consciousness. And then this should be able to assist the soul in making a much more comprehensive decision that is more akin to your soul. Because at this time you do not as yet have the full picture of what it is that is occurring with this implantation device.

Did David have a particular role on his star system?

Yes. When you are dealing with densities that are between fifth and sixth, the differentiation as we have here on this planet is much less than in those levels wherein the beings vibrate at a much more similar rate. There are certain individual differences, but it is not as widely divergent as the life forms upon this planet. This being chose to come forth to that particular system in order to bring certain knowledge, a certain ability to infuse into the energy grid work of that system to allow it to expand and evolve. Other beings chose to go elsewhere and do similar things in other systems. He was not necessarily the only one from his system doing this work, but that was his particular choice. When you move into seventh density level there is no longer a dichotomy as such of any type. There is only the movement in the Light, and further expansion along that track, shall we say. Not that there is any stagnation; there is always growth and movement of some type. Between fifth and sixth densities is the greatest possibility of this dichotomy occurring in consciousness. You have it here on your Earth plane in a very physical, graphic form, and perhaps that is one reason he chose this system to help, because his system is so much more advanced, and yet is also struggling with the dichotomy aspect. And so this would make it somewhat familiar, and it would provide a multi-leveled approach here on Earth because they are learning that lesson perhaps to a different degree upon his system; consequently, he would have much to contribute to a system that is undergoing a very similar thing, and is in the process of moving from one dimensional frequency into another, as is his system. Since there are so many steps beyond the Earth there is a great deal that this being has to offer in the teaching of the transmutations of these energies. It is seen that if the link to your system that is obstructing some of your frequencies at this time, if that is not adjusted properly, that will take a great deal away from you in a sense of being able to fully be here and to fully allow your abilities to function fully and completely here because you are kind of split almost, or torn, because your energies are not synchronized. There is a very fine tuning here that needs to be adjusted so that you may be able to truly come forth into your own while you are here.

This concluded David's reading which was conducted in 1992. This was before the Earth started moving into a higher vibration and all of the events leading up to a shift in energies in December 2012. Interestingly, Light Workers are now being advised that the Dark forces need to move into the Light or make their transition through death before Planet Earth can truly move ahead into Fourth Density. David seems to be one of the experiments which involve the Light forces assisting the Dark forces.

Chapter 10
A Hybrid Experiment

Roger would like some information and/or confirmation that he has had an extraterrestrial encounter in this lifetime. First of all, when was the encounter?

I get age seventeen.

How old are you now Roger, twenty-seven?

It is seen that this being has been used in what you would term a hybrid type of experiment.

Does that involve an implant?

It involves much more than an implant, per se.

Can you elaborate on what was exactly done in these experiments?

In this particular case, it is seen that there has been some type of device. There has been a different frequency inserted through the etheric vehicle. There is much agitation and the energies are not compatible at this time. There is a darkness in the field which is not indicative of a spiritual growth process, but rather a confusion of energies. There are two very distinct frequencies within this being, and they are in opposition.

Let me be sure I understand this. Is this like an implant that was placed in the etheric vehicle?

If by implant you mean more than just a simple device, per se, yes. If you would wish to include the range of energetic transplants, shall we say, almost surgically implanted, yes; then we would use the word implant. But if you would use it only to specify a type of device, no; this is not what is seen today. If it is, we do not see it localized anywhere, because the overall effect is overall. It is not just in one specific area; the entire field has been affected. And there is much molecular agitation in this being because of this frequency. One might almost call it an invasion.

Can you identify the beings that did this experiment on him?

These beings are not of what we would term of the higher spiritual realms. They are from a civilization which certainly is technologically far advanced to your present Earth lineage, but they are not in the Light. All are of the Light, but they are not in the Light in the sense that they have no understanding of the other facets of human nature, such as the emotional and spiritual vehicles *(meaning auric bodies).*

Is there anything Roger can do about this? It does not sound like a positive thing.

If this being allowed himself to come around a certain set of tonal frequencies, some beyond the human ear range to be applied two or three times daily. The vibration, the field that is within the being is like a crust in a sense. It's like someone poured concrete around this particular energy pattern. The frequencies which would be necessary to change this would then break it off. It would break it and dissolve it, so there would be no more hold on the field. It is seen that this would have to be experimented with a being that has the equipment to generate frequencies. There are machines on the market. An oscilloscope is one type of device that can at least register certain frequency rates. But then a device is necessary to be able to produce them so that the being can be engulfed by these frequencies. Two to three weeks it is seen would be sufficient to break up this field.

There is a ceiling in the energy field which has been placed there. It is a steely vibration. When trying to look beyond a certain level you hit this "poof" with a thud. It is a hard frequency that has been placed there as a device to shield and to hide.

Who are the beings that are causing these physical kind of happenings in Roger's body?

They are not what you would term physical, per se. Their life form is not physical. It is an interdimensional contact. It is difficult to get because it is shrouded. All I can get right now is they are interested in interdimensional species swapping. With the frequencies which are implanted they hope to not only gain an understanding of this species on this planet, but they in a sense transport themselves through this person. The twitches and all that this young man is referring to are but one of the many methods that these beings utilize.

A lot of so called extraterrestrials have equipment, if you will, where they study human beings and other species. They invade the energy fields, but they do not themselves put their energy through into those they study. This particular group in a very strange way that we have not encountered before put their energy, their own essence, at least part of their essence, through the beings that they are dealing with. It is almost a form of possession, and yet it is not, because it doesn't deal with Earth plane type of possession. It is not your typical possession because we are dealing with a very different type of energy here, and yet they are impinging upon this being's energy field. In order to get a much broader picture, it would be necessary to attempt to look at the soul contracts, the soul origins, etc. of this being, because this is not just something that has simply happened in this lifetime. There is a reason. Something happened in the consciousness of this being that has changed the whole molecular structure on a certain level. This young man has a greater ability, a more expansive awareness of time, but not as you understand it. It is like he is pulled back and forth almost between two time frames.

Are these beings he is involved with what we would call the greys?

Yes and no; not in the sense of what you understand them to be. They do not belong strictly to that classification. Yes, in the sense of grey meaning not quite of the Light. This is a very different species. This is one that is interdimensional. It does not show itself in physical form as a rule. They can if they wish, materialize, but they have no need or desire to do so. Because their study deals with human beings on this planet, and their laboratory is the energy fields of the humans that they have picked, and the contracts have been made, etc. They are on one level trying to live themselves, through the energy fields in this particular case of this young man. They are trying to understand the behavioral patterns, the frequencies, the energies, etc. etc. of what goes on in a human body without themselves coming into this realm through the normal processes. This in itself is a violation of universal cosmic laws. For that reason alone it would be advisable to take steps to eradicate this. No matter what the sensations, no matter what the drama may come with it at times; it is not worth it in the long run because the being is presently stopped in his own spiritual growth. What he is getting is an expansion of certain knowledge, but there is a missing factor, the missing link of the spiritual realm. These beings do not have an awareness of this.

Could we go back to the contract? Could we find out why Roger allowed a contract like this to be made?

We have here a scene of some smallish-looking extraterrestrial beings. They appear to be about three to four feet in height. And there is a taller being here. We don't know who is who here. We are just seeing this scene. And there is much discussion between this taller being and the smaller beings. All the others are all of the same size primarily. It appears that this being had an existence, perhaps several, in another realm in a so-called extraterrestrial capacity. And these small beings are having a discussion with the larger being because the larger being is so different from them. They are all alike. It is almost as though they were cloned from one source. This being was very different in appearance, and yet he was communicating with these small beings in this scene that we are viewing. The smaller beings are very curious. They wish to know how he got like that and what he's made up of and all these types of things. We feel a certain love from the being to these other small beings in this scene. Because of that bond the being wished to allow the other beings to study its life force. And so it allowed this opening to occur.

There have been many cycles. As the result of some of these experiences, and perhaps some ones in this life, there is an energy current in particular in the being that is totally blocked, and this is the one that leads to the spiritual self. It leads to a certain level of self-awareness. By that we do not mean on a physical level necessarily, but on greater and greater inner levels. This is blocked in large part because of the dealings with these life forms. But the choice was made to allow the experimentation to occur because the being had some kind of emotional connection at some other point in existence with other life forms. These life forms have gone on in their evolution and now they no longer present physical forms. They merely go through physical forms and work on and within other physical forms, which is really not according to universal law. These beings feel they have the right. They are not aware of any infractions of any laws because the agreement was made not under any kind of coercion. They feel they have the right since the agreement was made, and the opening was made, and they have the right to continue. However, the being himself, in order to effectively close this down must open to a level of self-awareness which is initiated through techniques and teachings that allow one to gain greater self-awareness. It is seen that this is a very vital point for this being if he truly wished to change this, and to alter this agreement which was made through a level of trust and through a level of a certain kind of love. It was not made under duress, and so there is almost a greater hold. And yet because of the difference in frequency between the Earth plane existence and these other life forms, there is a great deal of agitation and molecular disarrangement which is not conducive to this being's peace of mind. It is up to this young man himself to develop sufficient self-awareness, to bring that Light through that channel because unless that is done the agreement will continue. And he will basically be, in a sense, at the mercy of these forces. Now we are not saying this is evil, per se. This is just the level of ignorance from another realm which does not follow certain cosmic laws. None the less, it is not conducive to this being's spiritual welfare. It is only conducive to his fulfilling his agreement.

Has Roger had many Earth cycles, or is he relatively new to the Earth realm?

There have been Earth cycles as well. This being has had what you might term a well-rounded number of cycles. He has had many extraterrestrial types of existence and a number of Earth plane existences. This is not a being that has recently come to this plane. He has probably had almost like half and half, you might say, of the extraterrestrial and the Earth plane variety.

I am wondering if Roger has been given any particular knowledge or any particular gifts in this lifetime as the result of his allowing these beings in his space.

There is an understanding of different time frames and the ability to have a certain, unusual form of telepathic communication. At this time we do not see any particular aspect which stands out. Primarily what we see is the darkness. To penetrate this darkness, the message is that it requires this being to develop self-awareness to bring the Light through. It is not to be viewed as a battle, per se, because this was an agreement. This was not something that was forced upon you, even though the consciousness may have its doubts. But on the other hand, it is not something that your soul would wish to continue. You may still gain abilities and knowledge without having this type of exchange. There can be other realms of growth which you have not yet experienced. To have had that type of love that we have seen from that existence indicates a certain level of spiritual awareness in the past. It indicates a certain spiritual consciousness. So that makes it more likely that these beings have simply plugged up the channel for their own ends, for their own study.

(Addressing Roger) Is there anything that you have heard that particularly strikes you?

Roger: The telepathic thoughts stand out.

How do you feel about that ability?

Roger: It is an invasion of my privacy. It is as though somebody is reading my brain waves. Athor had talked about being able to block it through various frequencies three times a day. I would like to follow up on that.

This young man was 27 at the time of the reading. He was still living at home, being unable to hold down a job. His father brought him for the reading because he wanted clarification of what was going on with Roger. We hope that he indeed followed through on Athor's suggestions.

Chapter 11
A Soul from another Universe

We would like to start with the source of this soul. Dick has had much difficulty going into a past life situation or even back into this life. There seem to be some strong blockages. So we would like to get some information on those blockages and the birth of this soul.

We have here a scene wherein there are energies which take form and then they seem to be formless as they move in and out in certain patterns. There is one particular energy which seems to separate itself from this pattern of energy and Light, and it appears to be this soul consciousness. This particular Light seems to shoot upwards at a very rapid rate of speed, and as it does so it gives forth small particles of itself as though shedding these various little particles, but each one of them is a pin point of Light as well. It seems that this particular soul Light that we are reviewing seems to be in a great hurry as it wishes at this point that we are viewing to get back to the source. Yet the experience that it has chosen indicates that this was not going to be in such a fashion as it had seen through the soul's eyes, you might say. These pin points of Light and these energy fragments which are given off have settled on a plane, and they are mingling with that particular plane. This is not the Earth plane. There is a feeling in the vibrational frequency from this soul Light that it does not wish to be encumbered, that it wishes to get to where it is going. It has a very strong inner sense of purpose, motive and direction. And it appears that the lesson that it chose to learn from the onset, you might say, is one of a conflicting state almost at the onset of its differentiation from the source. The conflict was that it wished to return, and did not wish to be encumbered along the way. It saw that any additions to its energy field, any expansions, were an encumbrance. It wished to strip down to the nitty gritty. We will follow this soul Light.

It has come through to a plane where it has taken on a form of a rather large and powerful being. This appears to be one of the sub levels of the angelic kingdom. This is what you would term your mythology of the gods. This being we are viewing is very autonomous at this stage that we are viewing. And it is in a position of power; it delegates tasks to other energy forms. It seems to assist in helping these energy forms evolve because of the nature of its own particular frequency and consciousness at this time we are viewing. There is still this strong feeling of autonomy, and yet it is most difficult to describe in words. It is like the vibration in the frequency which was around the soul when it first differentiated from the source was one of great purpose, power and direction. However, this did not return it fully to an undifferentiated state which is what the soul had believed it would return to. There is a very deep misunderstanding from a soul level because the soul felt that it would return and yet it did not. It had to experience this autonomy which was not difficult for it in a certain sense. There was a conflict because the desire to reunite was extremely strong. And so the soul has a memory of feeling gypped, of feeling that somehow the forces have been against it. And this memory has lingered for eons of time. We see here that the being chose to differentiate for this particular lesson of learning how to cope, although cope is not exactly the right word, but it is the closest we can come to understand the many different parts of creation, of reality, of life on many different levels. If this soul does not achieve or accomplish what it feels it must then there is a great inner sense of frustration.

It is seen that in this existence we are viewing, the being had a very nurturing quality that it demonstrated by helping these energy forms evolve. It was like an overseer or guide of those beings of that plane. Then we see that the soul Light dropped and went into another evolutionary strain from there. It appears that the next phase it went into was a type of reverse polarity which is not known upon your Earth plane. The closest approximation would be some of the negative manifestations of what some beings or many beings of your planet would term as negative manifestation, but this is very different from the Earth plane. This is simply on an energy level, so we are not necessarily speaking of negative and positive, but that is the closest example that can be presented to this particular stage of evolution. At this phase the soul had to go to this particular universe in order to take on certain energies and to clothe itself with a certain density. Because its frequency and direction was so strong it gave off a frequency which would not allow it to attract other types of energies and clothe itself with any further density.

What is the relationship to the negative energy you are talking about?

It is what we term a reverse polarity. We are speaking of another universe, and the being had to do this in order to attract certain denser energies around itself, because the frequency it was giving off was so strong against any encumbrance that in order for it to evolve it had to do this. It is almost like anti-matter. It is very difficult to describe.

We haven't had a case like this before!

Dick: I understand what you are saying.

Good! (I still don't understand, but it is more important for the client receiving the reading to understand.)

From this place we see a type of explosion of energy. This explosion was most curious because the soul Light is not your typical explosion wherein the particles go in many different directions and are attracted elsewhere. This had its own orbit in this explosion of energy. There was a circumference around which the particles remained. And there was a most curious pulsating type of effect which occurred as a result of this explosion. This is still in another universe. There was this type of energy motion contracting and expanding, contracting and expanding, but all within a certain orbit. There was no energy lost, and it did not travel anywhere else. It was contained within this certain orbit. It is almost as though if it reached either edge of the orbit it would be propelled back, but as it was propelled back the energy acquired greater mass, greater density each time. Now we see that the energy has compacted into a very small ball. The ball is very dense. There seems to be anti-matter, or perhaps a black hole. It is uncertain, but this ball of energy is the most concentrated form of energy that can be imagined. It is almost as though the being having had that strong soul desire to return to the source, did it in this fashion, by becoming the most dense, compacted form of energy that is known in probably almost all the universe. It became quite inert, and yet the soul Light which vivified the inert mass of energy was very much not inert. It was very much aware. And so it had this experience of what is called the Black Hole, but it is the most compacted form of energy and in fact a return to the All That Is, but in a slightly different fashion. It was able to fulfill that desire and that need at that time, although not quite in the manner in which it had perhaps envisioned.

Now we see the soul Light then went back to the angelic plane. Here we see a scene where this soul Light was one of the beings which was involved with your upheaval on that plane wherein there was the beginning of the forces of Light as opposed to the forces of darkness, and it wished to experience this particular aspect of existence. So there is a strong memory within the soul consciousness of the forces of good and evil. This comes from that memory wherein there was that duality, and that splitting off of the force which again was a further experiment of the All That Is; nonetheless, for each soul consciousness this became an important factor that many became almost entrapped in. We now see a scene where the being is still part of the Devic Kingdom, angelic realm which comes to a place which appears to be what your beings term The Garden of Eden. We do not see a physical form but there is yet this angelic energy which is sort of overseeing this particular energy frequency and plane. Again there is this quality of protectiveness and nurturing quality which comes forth from the soul Light and it is very strong in this being – a loving, nurturing quality. The descent into matter was one of great displeasure to this being. The memory is quite blocked off because the feeling aspect of distaste was most pronounced as there was a sensation of great loss and further encumbrance as the energies which had to be encapsulated, and the being had to become one with a very slow rate of frequency. So there is this memory of extreme distaste as the being spent much time in both the angelic kingdom and other realms which were not physical, and not even in this universe. So there is this sense of darkness and fear. It is though there is a void and a vacuum in the consciousness because of the nature of the feeling aspect of the being in reference to these experiences.

In "Cosmic Relationships" I followed my soul Light from the source through many bizarre experiences, including being involved in 'The Fall' from the Angelic Kingdom. This came as a shock to me, and really difficult to believe. It was reassuring to discover another soul with a similar experience, a man who is highly successful in Earth terms but wanting to understand himself at a soul level. Dick was not able to go into a hypnotic trance. This reading explained why he has mental blocks, making it difficult to uncover his own soul records. As with so many of these readings, *I tried to tie the information into the present lifetime.*

Chapter 12
Destruction of Planet Maldek

We would like to trace this soul from the Source.

We have here a scene wherein there are multiple lights which appear to be a golden white hue. And one might say these lights are dancing. There is a particular unit of two balls of light which seem to be joined in the center in somewhat of a figure eight configuration. This particular unit of two balls of light disengages from the other group of lights. We will follow it. It continues on in its so-called travels, seeming to take what humans might term, time, although there is no such thing as time in these dimensions. But in viewing it from a somewhat linear, more human perspective, this is what we wish to say. And so it goes from place to place to place. It simply moves intra-dimensionally.

Now we have a scene wherein these two balls of light are now separating. The two seem to take root in some type of life form which in not something that is commonly known on this planet. Both of these lights take root in the same type of life form, just on a different part of this planet. And they grow into these columns of light. It would be similar to the Earthly trees, although this is not a physical plane dimension.

These columns of Light take root somewhat like a tree. The one here on the left goes way up into the stratosphere, and it seems to funnel out in a very large arc, and there are further forms of light that come forth from it, almost like a corkscrew of Light that goes up and through many other planes. In looking at it, that particular form has the appearance of a tornado in a funneling type of action. But it is still a light, an energy of Light, but it has a great velocity. In this funneling action the Light seems to draw unto itself certain elements from other dimensional plane frequencies

63

which it then funnels down through the funnel, and then comes down through the column of Light into that particular sphere grounding it.

There is a long discussion about this Light which I am skipping because it is quite involved. Is the light you are viewing the soul of Jane?

Yes. The other Light seems to have gone on its own journeys from this point on.

Would this other Light be like her twin soul?

Yes and no.

Please explain.

It is seen that the particular ball of Light which split off at some point in the evolution of this particular soul rejoined and then split off many, many times. This was primarily in the non-physical realms that this occurred. It is almost like a part of this soul sent a part of itself out scouting, to do research, to do messenger service, to learn many different things, and then to bring that information back to this particular soul life. And so to call it a twin flame in the manner in which beings on the Earth plane normally understand that terminology is not correct in this particular instance.

Now we see the Light and it is almost like a sea creature, a jellyfish or stingray. When it swims, it has a wonderful undulating motion. It is extremely sensitive, receptive, etc., but it is taking from the essence of that sphere and is trying to get a complete understanding of what these energies are that it is interacting with. This, of course, is not a physical plane, nor is it a human plane.

Now the energy moves up, and the mist is coalescing again into a more solid unit of Light energy. It vaguely resembles a squid type of Light energy. Now we see it streaking across the heavens and it alights in this place wherein there are two moons. It does not have the radiance of the daylight of the planet Earth. It has the silvery, bluish, blackish type of coloration in the atmosphere, so there is a very different type of lighting.

We see there are rather small beings. They appear to be between three to four and one half feet tall. The energy of this soul Light does not have the form of these other beings. It still has this almost squid like form, and at this point it is simply observing these beings. The beings are like worker drones of some type, and they are mining substances from both the surface and underneath the surface of this place. It is the Maldek system.

It would appear that the being at that time had very advanced telepathic and kinetic abilities. It was like one of the overseers of this group. It basically gave orders that were followed out by others. They are primarily a mining colony, and they were drone type workers. They were not extremely advanced, and it does not appear that they had any great individualized consciousness.

Now we are seeing a rather strange image here which would indicate that either at that point, or slightly before that point in the soul's evolution there is an attachment. We are not certain where the attachment came in, but it is quite certain there is an energy attachment here because in reading the record up to this point, this is what we are seeing. And the attachment developed from that system.

Maldek?

Yes, from the density of that system, because this energy form does not appear to be entirely of this being that we are reading, the lady in question.

We are trying to understand why there is this oppressive energy, and there is simply darkness. This is most pervasive. We are having difficulty getting through it. We cannot see any pictures, nor do we see the soul Light or anything after this experience. It appears that in the destruction of that system, the system itself involved many different frequencies and energy fields around it. This was not just one planetary sphere. This involved quite an extensive area. There is something about the destruction that occurred there. It did not simply happen as a result of what occurred on the surface of this system. It is seen that there was a most peculiar energy form, and this is what we are experiencing. It is a most peculiar energy source, a life form which had something to do with the destruction of this system. It is a life form.

The only way we can begin to describe this life form is that it is similar to what your scientists term a black hole; but it is a life form. This life form had the peculiar capacity of sucking in whatever it came near, and this had a very, very large proximity and radius. And so it would suck it in like a black hole type of thing. In a sense it would shred the frequency ranges. It would shred the atomic structure and would shred the subatomic structures. It would shred all the structures of the energies with which it came into contact. And it would annihilate them in a sense so that the consciousness, as we know it, was no longer present. There are not images except for the feeling, the most peculiar feeling of this life form. And so it is seen that the lady's soul Light was one of those that was sucked in by that life form within the Maldek system.

It is seen that as a result of that experience with this life form it spit out certain energies. It would release those energies which it could not fully digest. And so it is seen that the soul Light of the Jane being was one of those things that it spit out because it could not digest it nor shred it. And so the Light at that point was joined with the other Light of its own soul. So instead of there being two Lights at that point there was only one. There is in the depths of the consciousness of this Jane being the memory and recollection of this experience. Now the soul Light is well above the surface of this sphere that we are seeing. Again it seems to want to understand, comprehend, and exchange but it does not appear to be quite ready to experience anything with any greater density.

Was Jane in a physical body on Maldek?

It is seen that the entire reading of this soul's origin is going to more than likely be mainly on a non-physical level. We will try to reel it forward to an existence that is more tangible, shall we say.

We have here a scene wherein there is a very beautiful humanoid-looking being who appears to be of the feminine gender, almost an Amazonian type, larger than normal humans. This again does not appear to be totally physical. It is more a semi-solid, more etheric form. This being is simply walking on the surface of this place we are viewing. She picks up what appeared to be rock type formations; it actually appears to be on the moon. The rock type formations that are picked up are of a lunar type appearance of the rocks found on the moon. But there is some scenery there. It is not a stark bleak place where this being is. We do not see any other beings. This is a somewhat solitary experience. We believe that in seeing any further views of this soul Light, it would simply continue on in similar cycles.

Are there any other systems this soul Light visited?

This soul has had some experience with Venus. There have been what appears to be a cluster of experiences in the Sagittarius system of the constellation of Sagittarius.

This being has had a fair number of life cycles on this planetary system of Earth. This soul's consciousness is still searching for something. It does not know what it is searching for exactly, but there is a deep inner sense and conviction that it must reunite in greater totality with the other part of its soul Light, not immediately at the transition from this physical plane in this life cycle. At some point beyond that it is seen that there will perhaps be four to five more Earth cycles before the being will complete and ultimately continue on beyond the Earth plane dimension. And in these four to five coming cycles that this being has before it, there is much activity. It is seen that the being will be very concentrated in its life cycles. They will be cycles of service and great activity, and at the end of which, the being will have completed and fulfilled itself. At the moment of transition in this lifetime there will be many beings coming to meet and greet this one. In former life cycles this being has dealt with many, many individuals. It has had lifetimes of great power. It has also had lifetimes of great tragedy; but many of the beings it has dealt with are on the other side, so they will be greeting her in the transitional period. This is most interesting because there is a whole slew of beings that are just waiting and very happy to assist, etc. That is not something we commonly see.

As usual I concluded the reading by asking if there was any particular message to Jane from the Sirian Counsel of Twelve. There ensued a long discussion of some particular spiritual exercises she could do. These are meant for this individual exclusively, so have been deleted; but the final words can be applied to all souls.

Always look to the highest of the totality of All That Is, so you do not get hung up on one aspect which may be but a brief second of time in the scheme of cosmic time cycles. In viewing your soul's history, please remember that the things which were spoken of were just a brief second in time. You have had many, many other cycles in the physical and the non-physical, and in other systems. Your soul will continue growing, expanding and reaching forth into the cosmic oneness of All That Is. There is never an end to evolution. Please do not forget this. You will not end. You essentially had no beginning as do none of us. It is a continuum, an infinite continuum, and we are most thankful that you have provided us this opportunity to view your particular life on this continuum. We wish you well, and send our love and blessings. Thank you.

Chapter 13
A Being from Maldek and Andromeda

We would like to trace this soul from the Source.

We have here a scene wherein there is a kaleidoscope-type of reflective lights going in and out. And there are many multi-coloreds, almost rainbow colored lights. There appears to be a scene of a being on a table. Whether this is the actual first differentiation or not, we are not certain, but this is what is coming at this time. The being has humanoid features, but it is much taller than the average human being, and rather slim. There does not appear to be hair on the body, and the being has a grayish, bluish tinge to the skin which is of a different substance than the human skin. The skin has no pores, it would seem, and the being is also bald. There is no hair on the head; the eyes are sunken in - they are just round orbs, sunk way into the head. The forehead protrudes considerably compared to the average human, as does the frontal lobe area, and the top of the skull. The back of the skull protrudes considerably compared to the human skull.

So we have here a being that is approximately seven and a half feet tall with unremarkable muscular structure that does not appear to be any particular muscular configuration anywhere. The limbs are equal; both legs and arms appear to be almost the same. There is no protrusion of any hip area, per se.

Now the lights which we are viewing are above the body of this being. It does not appear that the being is what you would term physically dead, just in some type of almost catatonic state. And these lights are designed to help either heal or awaken it - something of this type. So we see finally the being is getting off of this table area. It walks over to get dressed. There are smaller beings in this place, and they help

71

this taller being get dressed. The being is giving orders to the smaller beings.

Now the being goes outside. This is a rather unusual looking place outside, for it is quite dark. There is some kind of light source but it does not appear to be like a sun. It is more like a light source from some type of moon. There is something in the sky that is slowly burning up, and that is producing a faint light source for this area. The area appears to be quite barren; there is no vegetation. It is a rocky, somewhat hilly terrain. The being is now getting into some kind of craft. It would appear that the being was getting energized for a journey to another system. Basically it is sort of like what a camel does when it drinks a lot of water and stores it for a desert trek. The being was doing this with the energy of these multi-colored lights because it would not have the type of substance it was used to, and it would need an extra boost, etc.

For some reason this is a very small craft. The being has two assistants. It is not going in a large craft, and evidently the ones that were helping it dress are the ones that are going on this mission. It is seen that the being travels like with a time warp factor; and that is another reason the energy from the lights was necessary, because the mode of traveling could make it difficult on these beings. There appears to be a difficulty here. It is almost like the being got lost in this inter-dimensional passageway. It is difficult to find the right words, because what we are seeing is like an energy storm that is like dimensions folding in on each other; and there seems to be rapid movement. There was a molecular transformation that occurred in this type of travel. It created quite a stir in the psyche of this being. It would seem that this was not the first time the being had traveled in this manner, but there was a difficulty of some type in the particular journey

The being finally arrived at a place which was quite different; it is a sunny place, very similar to Earth. There are many life forms growing there. The plant life forms are quite different from Earth life forms. They appear to be of semi-sold substance. The being went to confer with some of the life forms on that system. We see that there is some type of a council there that the being went to meet. It was a representative from its system, and it came because its system was dying out. It came with a lot of questions and information. The beings from its system at that time wanted to strike up some kind of agreement, to bargain with this other system so that they would not die out. They were trying to gain scientific knowledge and understanding of the life forms on this other system and how to adapt. It seems that this was the closest place to where they were located. Their planet or star, being so barren, etc. was like in its dying throes. It had been like that for some time, but the beings could no longer adapt to this type of needed Light. They needed the energies and frequencies of Light. This is one of the reasons the machine was utilized on this being before it left, because it was their source of food and fuel.

There was some kind of difficulty in coming to a sufficient agreement. There was something that this council did not like about this species and they felt a little threatened. So they basically did not open up completely, and it was a very tentative agreement. Basically it indicated that they would be quarantined, and they would not be allowed to move about freely on this new system until the council had decided that it was indeed safe, and their life forms did not in any way threaten the civilization on that system.

It seems that this being has a very strong ET connection of many cycles in which she was both an explorer and a spokesperson of sorts for various beings in a particular system. Many times this had to do with research, with furthering the development of her own particular species and her own particular system. She is well versed in this leadership type role and capacity. She is again seeking to make a fuller contact and connection. It is like she wants to complete a circuit, a cycle. This system we have just viewed is of the Andromeda system. There has been an ongoing connection with that species, with their beings. She has been an ambassador from one species to another.

We will look for other cycles. Evidently it is going back to that cycle again. It is seen that the beings moved out of that dying system and went into this new system. However, she felt that she had been betrayed by one of the beings on the council of that system because there seemed to be some kind of personal interaction that perhaps they had had other cycles elsewhere together, and there was a basic distrust between them.

There were perhaps one or two hundred of her beings who migrated to Andromeda. The others were not able to sustain life and had reincarnated. This was a very heavy burden, in a sense, because there was within the being a feeling and a sense that somehow she must revive this species. She felt she needed to bring forth greater numbers of this race so they could again flourish; but the problem was they were in another system, and the distrust between this council member and this being was such that there was not freedom. There was no ability to expand and to allow her beings to colonize the new system. They were simply not in a position to do that. They were guests of this place, and this did not satisfy this being who had designs and plans to further her own civilization.

Something occurred between the group of her beings and some of the other beings that were watching over them and keeping them in close quarters and somewhat confined. There was a skirmish, and many of the "hosts" were killed because this group decided to break free, and so there was a battle. They took off in ships and they found a segment of the planet that was not so inhabited and they landed there. It is seen that they colonized there. They were not followed because this part of the planet was uninhabitable by the other beings. It was very rough terrain and there was a darkness over this part of the planet. This was more familiar terrain to them and they could thrive in this much better than the other beings. And so they colonized there. They settled and grew in numbers. Basically they flourished. There was sufficient Light for them to begin to grow and harvest things. They had the ability to materialize from certain substances, from the ethers. They couldn't materialize everything but there were certain things they could create from virtually nothing except an energy source. So they built and developed a whole civilization. It appears that the system they left was Maldek, which had been destroyed.

Everything was fine as long as they could stay there on this part of the planet they came to, but it is seen that one day finally some ships came from the other beings, and there was warring that occurred there. Both sides lost many beings. However, this being was quite hardy and quite cunning; it escaped by going further underground there. They had developed some passage ways and systems which allowed them almost to go to the core of that system. And they had manufactured instrumentation so that they could subsist if necessary deep underground in the Andromeda system.

There is some connection, some underground caves, tunnels, whatever somewhere through Colorado *(this client lives in Colorado)*. If the being has not found them yet, it is seen that there will be some kind of memory in the psyche of this being. The memory will begin to surface that there is something she needs to investigate. She is looking for her own kind, we hear. There is a strong presence and intelligence of this ET being and yet there is a physical vehicle and a physical form which is interacting here on Earth. The real consciousness is not so much that of a human as it is of this type of being. There have evidently been many cycles on other systems wherein the being has had leadership roles and capacity.

Much time went by and the being continued to exist underground with a few beings around it, essentially while the war raged on above ground. They never resurfaced because there was so much radiation as a result of this battle. They knew they would not be safe so they basically stayed ensconced underground. The being never resurfaced in that cycle. It basically just left the form behind at the moment of what you would call physical death. There is such a strong connection with that cycle that we would strongly recommend that she undergo some type of past life recall work with someone who can guide her into this so that these energies can be released and reintegrate.

From that existence it is seen that the being went through much more finer levels of energetic types of existences. It felt on one level that it had lived so long through that form because that form basically had to go underground and had to live a kind of imprisoned life again. It did not wish to be limited in this way again, so for quite some time the being simply went into energy forms of existence in various realms wherein it learned much about frequencies and energy currents. It would be basically impossible to describe these in any great detail because there is no precedence on Earth to these types of existences. We would have to have a mathematical language to more adequately describe what actually occurred and so we will leave it at that.

This was a long, fascinating reading. The next part goes into a completely different existence, which is more appropriate for a separate chapter.

Chapter 14
Existence as a Dinosaur

This is a continuation of the above reading.

We have here what appears to be an egg. From this egg we see a life form that would be similar to a dinosaur type. This does not appear to be Earth. These life forms were highly intelligent beings, but they were predatory. The intelligence was put more into the area of cunning for survival. The intelligence of that species was not the type of intelligence that was utilized for philosophical type of speculation but it was more of a raw intelligence, a cunning that allowed them to survive as a species. They had a very interesting social structure wherein there was great love and caring for the off spring and others in this so-called family unit, somewhat similar to the wolves on planet Earth that have a very advanced social structure in their community. It is seen that because of the predatory nature of these life forms they basically killed each other off. The few remaining were transported. It is seen that they were taken, among other places, to Earth. It was mostly the eggs and the small younger ones that were left and removed to this other place where they would not be in such great numbers; therefore, there would be greater food for them to eat, and it would not be as difficult for them to survive because the prevalent food sources there would be sufficient to keep them going; they wouldn't just simply have to kill each other off type of thing. And so there was a great deal learned of survival in that existence. It is seen that the memories of this existence are housed in the lower chakras, particularly between the base and second chakra. There seems to be a wealth of information hidden within this lady and needs to be unblocked. Your soul wishes to make connections between all this, to understand yourself. We wish you well and thank you for the opportunity to be of service and to read your soul records. God bless and may you move further and further in the Light of the Oneness of All. Thank you.

The main purpose of <u>Book Two </u>*is to illustrate how the soul evolves from many life forms and how it is an on-going, never ending process. Freaky, strange and difficult to believe, I know, but vital to our understanding of our Creator- All That Is. The dinosaurs as well as all other animals are actually our ancestors. They are part of the long evolutionary process of souls. This is before the souls become individualized, since animals are part of group souls; and perhaps people are attracted to certain animals because they have inhabited one of those particular bodies before it became a human.*

Chapter 15
One of the Founders of Sirius

This client was a former Catholic nun, but she began questioning many of the teachings of the Church. She would like to know about her soul origin- the point of differentiation, and particularly her connection with Sirius.

This is a very beautiful scene. The closest we can come to describing it is if you look into a kaleidoscope and see all these colors coming forth, and just flowing in various patterns, etc. Now we see a star. It appears that this is either symbolic or representative in some fashion of the Sirian system. Perhaps it is the actual point of differentiation, but this is not in any type of physical or semi-solid form. The star just shows. We are moving through an energy field that moves very quickly. It is almost like a tunnel of energy. Perhaps it is an interdimensional gateway. Now we are just experiencing traveling rather than any arrival at a specific so-called destination. It is like you are in a time warp. You are in a zone wherein there is an energy that permeates everything around the being. And this energy has both a sucking, pulling, pushing, implosive type of impact.

It appears that you have had many, many existences, many of which were in what would be termed interdimensional space and going through interdimensional gateways. There seems to be an element within this being of an osmosis quality. It was able to flow, to merge, to move in and out, although getting sort of stuck in that tunnel was not our idea of what we are talking about now. The being has had a lot of existences in this type of state where it flowed, united, became one, etc. with whatever was its experience. This, of course, was non-physical. It is also almost devoid of shape. It could take on a form, although it did not keep it. This being is what we would term an ancient soul.

What is her connection to Sirius?

We hear she is one of the founders of that system.

Does that mean she had a physical form there?

Yes and no; again in the aspect wherein a semi-physical form was necessary to deal with certain principalities, etc. But to say that the being resided in an etheric form, no. It was an energy unit, and always has been an energy unit that has experienced many, many different realms of existence.

We would like to thank you for coming here because we feel honored to have you.

Carmel: Part of my work in this life has been intercession, a word I use to describe the frequent experience where I suddenly take on physical, emotional or mental symptoms from the Earth and hold the energy temporarily to relieve it.

If you feel drawn to holding the Earth energy and working with that at this time then we would add that you visualize a beam of brilliant white Light coming from the star Sirius directly through you, around you, and containing you as well as filling you, going through you into the Earth, to the center of the planet wherein is the so-called Earth star, and you connect that beam of Light from the Sirian system to the Earth star, deep within the center of the planet. When this visualization is correctly performed by such a one as you, the resulting Light emanating from this connection will be magnificent, which is quite an understatement. This is the first founder of Sirius we have run across.

Carmel: Sometimes I would open my mouth and messages would come through. I would be shocked when I heard them because I had no clue. I just never knew what was going to happen either. People with Ph.Ds. in theology would tell me there was no way I would know that. It often happened when I worked with people. Things would come out, and I had no clue how to help them, and all these words would come out and they would get help, but I had no idea how that happened.

Something is trying to get a message across. It is a strong energy presence. Tell her not to worry. There is such a strong energy here of Light, of a bright light that is overpowering my ability to tune on individual names. (Carmel had asked a question about her sister whom she believed would soon be a soul exchange with her mother who had died in 1985.)

When Carmel initially came to my office and was introduced to Athor, she had tears in her eyes from the emotions she was experiencing. As stated, in our many soul readings, we had never before had a client who was a founder of Sirius. I would have liked to get more details about how that happened, but Carmel had a long list of questions and I felt the need to try and address them. Actually her first question was about her relationship with Jesus. The answer was quite long so will not be covered here, but the bottom line was she was a disciple, and had feelings of guilt because she felt she should have done something to prevent the death of Jesus. These feelings spilled over into future lifetimes and created blockages in her memory banks. Carmel had requested an Athor reading, but she was not one of my therapy clients. She had read From Sirius to Earth and felt a huge bond with Athor which was evident when the two met.

Chapter 16
Souls from the Pleiades and Andromeda

This chapter takes excerpts from two different readings. Both covered many soul issues, but for purposes of this book, only the sections discussing star systems are included.

Is there any particular star system John is connected to?

The Pleiades. Your cycles have been extremely varied from system to system, and even on the Earth plane itself. You have had a great deal of varied life cycles, so you have had much experience with many different systems and waves of life and living. This is much to your benefit, because it is seen that in this life not only will you have access to the angelic band of healing angels, there will be other beings that will come into your field and visit, so to speak. There are many beings from other systems that are awaiting a certain development in your evolution before they can make contact, but they are waiting. You are as messenger of certain cosmic concepts, and these cannot come forth fully until your development has reached a certain level. It is imperative that you continue whatever work you can in contemplation and studying in the spiritual paths as this will only further your evolution and your ability to bring forth very vital information which will help many other beings. We see that there are approximately fifty beings that you have had connections with in other cycles and other existences who hope to make contact.

This was a remote reading for a client in Iowa who later wrote a book. He was kind enough to send me a copy of his book. Apparently this reading was very helpful in his self-understanding. Earlier in the reading, one of the things he was told by Athor was to listen to the Hallelujah Chorus when he wishes to access the angels - something that might be helpful to others wishing to access the angels. All of the other information was of a personal nature that would apply only to John.

The next reading was for Ellen in Tennessee. She states that she feels no particular attraction to specific places on Earth or periods of history. "I often feel more like an observer of human events than a participant, in spite of being sought out by others as a mentor and confidant. I have often felt naïve and incompetent in dealing with human affairs as if this was all new to me. I am wondering if there is a possibility that I am originally from elsewhere, with only a few Earth incarnations."

It is seen that she is indeed from elsewhere. One could say there have been few Earth cycles, but the being partially experiences this feeling of being an observer from the locked, walled off energies (discussed earlier in the reading). That is only part of it. The other part is indeed because of the origins. There is a unique configuration in this being's make up which we have not seen before and it makes it very important. It is important that she get the appropriate guidance from beings that are sufficiently developed and good at what they do to guide this being properly.

Is there any particular star system that she has a strong alignment with?

We hear Andromeda.

I ask for any final words from the Sirian Council.

We have seen your progress through many, many cycles. We have seen you in off-Earth existences, and we have seen that you have a wealth of history in other systems of which you are as yet unaware. The time will come in the near future when as you work and progress on these emotional blockages you will begin to remember. This remembrance will be part of the path to your inner joy and inner happiness, that feeling of connectedness which you seem to lack. You are only lacking it simply because of these blocks. These energies are not in harmony with your Light, and as they are transmuted, these other memories of other existences will begin to grow. You will also begin to access these gifts from those cycles, which will make you feel much more complete and whole. We wish to thank you for the opportunity to read your records and we wish you well. God bless and God speed on your journey of Light.

Chapter 17
A Light Worker with an Existence Underground

I met Keland at a conference in Mt. Shasta. She requested an Athor reading from the Source.

We have here a scene wherein there is a very large, bright light, like a sun and the sun is pulsating. It contracts and it expands. There is a center within this sun. The center is like a nucleus of another type of Light. The sun appears between a goldish, whitish color and the nucleus that we are looking at has a bluish color with a white radiance around it. The nucleus within this central Light begins to pulsate very similarity to the sun; but the difference is, while the sun expands and contracts, it seems to radiate out almost in streams of Light, but they do not leave the central ball of Light. Now the nucleus is getting larger and larger and larger. This nucleus Light is a very, very large ship. We have never seen this before. The ship obviously has inter-dimensional qualities and properties. It can go and change dimensionally. It can shift and travel, but not in a linear fashion, not in the manner in which humans can understand space travel, but rather in an inter-dimensional form of traveling. This brain does not have the physical language of physics within its semantic vocabulary to be able to give you in words what exactly is occurring here, but we will do our best to describe this.

The ship is massive, but to use the term 'ship' does not do it justice. It is an energy unit of a world contained within this so-called flying saucer devise, and it contains many different categories of life forms. That would mean on one level it is a holding place for future colonization. This ship is a living entity actually as there are many different facets of what is going on within this ship.

We are trying to see a particular being, but we are just experiencing the entire organism. We would prefer to call this an organism, rather than a ship, although it has the functions of a ship. This organism has the capacity to colonize. It has the capacity to rescue. Please state your name again. Perhaps we can get a more singular unit.

I state the name again.

At this point we are simply seeing and experiencing this organism. It appears that in some way it is difficult, if not impossible, to describe that was your essence at that time; this organism that contained all these other life forms. Again there is this pulsating motion of expansion and contraction as though your essence was trying to learn to differentiate further. Now we have a scene where we have one smaller ship, and this ship goes off at a very rapid rate of speed into a galaxy which is not known here on this Earth. It is not in the Milky Way but is much further away. Somehow this ship later on has a connection with the Andromeda system. The connection seems to be from this whole unit which was differentiated into this living organism that was just huge. The whole organism went to the Andromeda system, but this one smaller ship had a reconnaissance mission. Now we see some forms that are humanoid in appearance. This is on the surface of what appears to be the moon or some similar planetary system. There are several humanoid looking forms. They appear to have some type of garments on, some type of space suit type things. This is very strange because what we are seeing here is an image very similar to present day astronauts. There are several of these beings on the surface of what appears to be the moon and they are communicating. Then they go off in different directions. There is some kind of gear and different machinery that they go to get. And they set up a strange looking devise on the surface of this place. This devise appears to be metallic in origin and very large. They have put it together because each of them has gone to their separate areas to retrieve the pieces that were needed and they brought them together. It appears to be some type of sending device. It also has the capacity to receive. We hear it both sends and receives signals and these signals are not only for the purposes of communication and broadcasting to far reaches but they also have something to do with doing the research on the surface of this place and potentially this device has the potential of changing some of the molecular structures on the surface of this place.

We see three beings in particular here doing this work. This device has three large metal prong type things and when they came together it is almost like a flower closing. But now as these tones and frequencies come forth from it, the thing starts opening up these metal claws and we see this unusual form of energy coming from within the center of this apparatus. This energy is not just simply a pure beam of light, there appear to be particles both coming from it, within it and coming into it as well. Part of this energy was powered through the beings and some of the devices they had on them. But this being comes through this energy field and materializes. He is giving directions to these three of what should be done next basically. This is the leader of this particular research group but he was elsewhere and so they basically brought almost like a holographic image of the being through this machine so that they could communicate. It appears that part of the message is that they are going to colonize this place. In the next scene there are ships and many beings coming. There is tremendous research being conducted so there are many ships that come with many beings who do various things, etc. The three here, including this being, finish their task and they get their data, compile it and then we see that this being goes off. They all have their individual jobs and this one goes off to her station. The being is pondering something very deeply. There appear to be some calculations that don't seem to come out right. They don't match up somewhere and there is something about these beings colonizing this place – a force field must be set up on the surface and around this planetary sphere to sustain the life forms. Now we see many beings keep coming and there is more research and more research. Pretty soon there is a first wave of colonization beings who start coming. We see many ships coming to this place; the beings get together and there is a meeting. This one here has spoken to some of the higher ups in this research group indicating that there could be some difficulties with sustaining their life forms because they didn't want to utilize equipment to breathe. The field has not been set up yet and so there is this big meeting where the beings are told that they need to go back because the machine to set up an energy field has not been balanced out yet.

And so they take off and this being is still there. She is just pondering and working very hard to figure out what the missing part of this is. We see that the being gives up because it cannot find the right combination in the formula. It becomes despondent and the image of being so tired and worn out that there is nothing left. We see the being lying down – there are slightly different types of feelings that these beings have. They have emotions, but it is a little different from humans and it would be very difficult to describe this difference unless the being can feel the energy. We see what appears to be like the soul Light coming forth from the being and going out trying to find a way because it felt very responsible. It had this job and it wished to make it right. It goes out in this realm and it communicates with a being we see is one of our Sirian Council members. This is part of the reason this one has had some of the feelings she has had in reading the Athor book.

She is communicating with the council member and receives the information and is able to make the changes in the calculations but there was the time factor. Because of certain cosmic cycles it couldn't just be adjusted and then suddenly everything was fine and the beings could colonize. It wasn't that simple so there was a long period of time. It was like the rotation of this planetary sphere needed to complete a certain cycle. The being had to leave the surface of that place because the cycle was too long and the being had to leave knowing that she had achieved the proper combination but not having been able to remain to see the end results of her work. And so there was a certain sense of loss because she had worked so hard and then had finally succeeded but then could not be there to see the end results of her efforts.

(Some time was spent assisting Keland in learning how to release this energy).

There is a being with a rather unusual looking headdress. It appears to be humanoid but not entirely. It is almost like the way the head is shaped. The head doesn't just close up like with human beings but it kind of just sprouts out; it bends outward in rays. This is strictly an etheric existence. There is a density and feeling to this so it is fairly solid in makeup. The being is just standing there and the head with all these streamers from the head which would almost appear like hair or a headdress, but is actually a part of the head. The being is just kind of slowly moving back and forth while it is standing there. It is almost like it is trying to acclimate to get used to certain energies or to feel and record certain energies around it in the atmosphere. So it is almost like the way the head is shaped, coming out like it does in these streamers, it is almost like a radar type device. It is sensing the surrounding atmosphere and the frequencies. Again it was like doing research and this is not its home base in that life form. It is gathering all of this data from this motion and the data is being transmitted to a ship. There is again an element of feeling that it hadn't completed again; it hadn't done enough. It has something to do with the sensory apparatus and this apparatus had almost a sense of smell, a sense of taste, of feeling, of everything. The being is aware that there are other senses and a greater more expanded way of sensing and feeling than that she has in a human body. Is that correct?

Keland: Yes.

The fact that you have come through the human frame has been one of your particular greatest successes. It is rather interesting because for you in many, many off- earth existences you did not find satisfaction; you did not find completion. For you the completion is through this dimension, by bringing together all that you have been and all that you have seen and done and unifying that within.

We have here a scene of what might be Earth. It is a very beautiful wilderness type place. It is a very beautiful place. There are maybe four or five beings playing in the water and having a good time. And there is one being that comes telling them to hurry. There is something important going on. The other beings appear to be teenagers or slightly older. So they are all excited wondering what it could be and so they get dressed and come out of the water. Now there is a gathering of many beings. Everybody gathered together for this meeting. And this one man appears; he is telling them that there is a coming cataclysmic event and this beautiful place where they live is going to be destroyed. There is a great, grave somber feeling that comes over these beings from this news. They ponder this greatly about what are they going to do. He is saying that if they go inside the mountain area, that they have a place prepared for this coming change. These beings have been in this beautiful place with brilliant sunshine, warmth, water, everything pristine, clear and clean. He is telling them that they must go underground. They realize that they do not have much choice if they wish to survive so they very slowly file into the mountain and go down very deep inside, almost one would say the bowels of the earth. There is a place prepared. We see that they have been given the choice, that if they go in there they will be allowed to change their form. If they do, they will become underground dwellers. They will go through a certain transmutation but they will generally maintain their usual form. If they choose not to go through that process, then they will be taken off the planet *(die)*. You had the experience and memory of that wonderful beauty and then this tremendous decision had to be made.

There are many, many cycles in your past experience wherein you have had to make very monumental decisions regarding your life form so that is an issue that weighs heavily on you at an energy level. There is a great heaviness within the psyche from these types of experience, particularly from the existence described because that was closer to the human emotional strata than the others.

What did Keland decide?

Each one made a different decision. Some decided to stay and they gradually mutated to become used to living underground but there was not the normal life source that they were accustomed to. Others went on into another realm. I hear Keland stayed. There is a great heaviness from that cycle and also from that decision. It is not so much that the being feels she should have gone but it was difficult having to adjust to that type of life form and the lack of the sunshine, etc. There was a combination of events that occurred that gradually changed this underground civilization so they

95

eventually merged and went into a different dimension so they were no longer strictly physical. However, that didn't happen overnight. That civilization is yet there in the Earth today. You can visit it. There is an area close to the Bimini area. That is a most brilliant place. If you attempt to go there, you will have many beautiful experiences.

I am assuming Athor means to go there and meditate. The transcript ends at this point. Every now and then I receive an e-mail from Keland giving me some "enlightening" information. She appears to do a great deal of traveling and seems to be spreading much "Light" in this lifetime. She was crying during the reading since it seemed to touch something deep within her psyche. It was a great privilege to meet such an advanced soul!

Chapter 18
A Light Worker Who is here to Assist in the Earth's Dimensional Shift

This is another reading for an advanced soul who is an engineer in this lifetime. Shelly had an amazing knowledge of physics. She took some quite technical material channeled by Athor about planets birthing into stars and changed it into more understandable information. She would often spend many nights looking up at the stars. She claimed to have had numerous sightings which were an inspiration to her. She requested a number of Athor readings over the time we knew her. This was a reading from the Source.

We have here a scene where there is a tremendous explosion of Light and it appears from a central sun. We are drawn into the center of this Light. As we go through the center of this Light, we are in a dimension that is a mixture between fluidic and gaseous. It is somewhat akin to being under water but not quite of the same density. We are moving through some type of membrane. This is another dimension. This being that appears has a fairly humanoid structure and appears to be swimming in this sea of energy. There are other beings there; these have the ability to sense through every pore of their forms. They draw in sustenance through every single cell and every pore. These beings have a tremendous delight. They are similar to the fairy kingdom, but this is a whole different dimension. They are of the air element but also a combination of elements. They are just so free and unbounded and yet there is form of some type although it is not physical. The beings do not seem to have the capacity for any negative emotions. They have a total trust and total innocence, much greater than any Earth child because they have had no karma as such and they have known nothing else except in this one's case she originated from the Source. It would appear that the others also had this experience; this is for many of them their first encounter in a form. It is a most exquisite dimension; however, because this is life in a Garden of Eden of sorts, there is no growth, no movement because everything is pretty much perfect you might say. There is no opposing force, no friction. The being certainly enjoyed being there. After eons have gone by some kind of a force impacts on that dimension. It creates a shift; with this shift it opens the dimensional doorway so that there is more permeability so other dimensions can come through and pass through more easily. The membrane between the dimensions thins. Here we have the beginning of friction. We have the beginnings of energy sources that have heretofore been foreign to this dimensional frequency. It is like total chaos occurs. The fluidic motion and the former structure is almost under attack because it has been hit by another frequency which is going to produce change. As a result of this dimensional shift it is seen that many of these beings were sucked into a vortex of energy. As a consequence they lost their forms because this was a whole different dimensional frequency. This was rather unpleasant because it came with what you might say a 'big bang'. It totally disrupted the status quo and the level of harmony, the total balance and peace.

Before you continue, what dimension is this?

The seventh. Now the being is becoming a ball of light and the ball is moving through many dimensional frequencies. It is seen that it has not chosen any particular form but is kind of traveling in a sense.

We have here a scene of what appears to be some kind of planet or star, but this is a very highly developed place. There are dwellings and beings in this city. It is a fairly dark place. The lighting is greenish, bluish, grayish kind of lighting.

These beings have almost amphibious skins or forms. They are not scaly, they are smooth and rubbery. They are very tall beings and they all look pretty much identical. The only differences are in the manner of the reflection of the consciousness and in the light which comes forth through their one central eye. In the light which comes forth from that eye there are different colors or frequencies which come forth which is the only individuality which we see here. These beings are concerned with what is commonly on this Earth termed higher knowledge. They are a race of beings who study what you might term the secrets of the universe. They are not concerned with food and clothing, concerns so prevalent on planet Earth. They spend their whole time with their full concentration on learning, on studying. In fact some of the thought frequencies of these beings and perhaps some of the seeds of these beings were carried to Earth. It is seen that the thought frequencies of these beings greatly influenced the one called Pythagoras and other mathematical beings upon this plane.

Is this a different galaxy?

Is it a planet or is it a star?

It appears to be a star system but does not have a name you would recognize. Now the light seems to be searching. Then we have another explosion of some type of light here. We see a very bright star. The light body chose to inhabit a system which was totally alien to the being. There is nothing on the Earth plane that would even remotely connect to it so there really are no words to describe this experience that this being had there. It acquired the capacity to evolve as an individuated essence from this place. There the soul matured to the level of when the soul light became strong enough and mature to the level of individual consciousness of its soul light. This was a big step.

The next scene we have is unusual. It seems to be very similar to an Earth body. There are images of a body lying in a room and there is a light bulb that is just swinging back and forth on the ceiling. How odd! Maybe this was a soul exchange because the person just kind of is out of it, disoriented and the light is swinging. It is difficult to find out what this is, because it jumps from a total alien system to what appears to be similar to an Earth body. There seems to be an unusual exchange to have made such a leap from that system to this image. It appears to be a male body and the being seems to have been interrogated or something and it was alone locked up in this room. Perhaps it is not so much that that the light bulb was moving but the person's perception when he was getting up. He was being interrogated because there had been a huge change in the person. The exchange or whatever had happened had just occurred a little while before this, and the person was trying to adapt; the senses were reeling. This was not from abuse. This exchange had been made from a totally foreign system. The soul dropped in and the light of this soul came forth through this body that we are viewing. The being is trying to get adapted. The senses are not working right yet and the being is not with it yet. We see the being is looking down at its hands and feet and its body. It just does not compute. There is a feeling of total shock. There has been no precedence prior to that and he is trying to understand what this is all about. This really is not clear. There is a possibility that this soul exchange is another aspect of the Shelly soul. Indeed that is the case. Prior to the exchange it had not had an Earth life. It appears that the being had been a missionary and the natives had grown quite weary of this being. The man had been put through much physical stress. It is seen that some years prior to that, it appears to be approximately five years prior to that scene, the being had come into this jungle community in the Amazon. He had befriended the natives and was what you might term a zealous missionary. As a consequence of this zealousness, some of the male members of the tribe were more than a little perturbed. It is seen that within two years of his arrival they decided to dispatch him. They took the man to an open pit and put four stakes on the outside of the open pit. They stretched the man and tied him with thongs to these four stakes so that his body hovered over this pit. It would appear to be a good fifteen to twenty feet deep. All that was supporting his body were the thongs holding his wrists and his ankles. They left him there; it rained and the sun came through – not directly because there was too much vegetation, but the humidity, the heat and the pain were quite devastating. It seems that this was the native's way of trying to exorcize his particular spirit. They felt he was full of demons. It appears he was like this for four or five days. Since it rained he did manage to get some water and fortunately the body did not die. The vipers in the pit were not able to come up the pit because the walls were too steep. So there was this psychological torture of knowing that death was just ten or fifteen feet below so he became quite delirious. It is seen that one of the women who had liked him and wanted to follow his ways, came and cut the thongs. It seriously damaged the shoulders and the back because he first cut the feet, and here was this big hole under him. He went backwards against the other side of the pit. He lost consciousness because his shoulders and back hit the wall. She managed with great difficulty to cut one arm, one hand, and one wrist then began to pull him up then cut the last thong. She got one of her children, a young boy, to help her carry this man off into the jungle. They built a little shelter for him and she came to nurse him daily until he recuperated sufficiently where he could walk and she warned him that he needed to leave and go far away. And so this is what he did.

We next see him some time since his ordeal. Because of the ordeal he had developed some kind of jungle fever. The fever made him quite disoriented. At the time when the exchange was occurring it was at a time wherein the body was not in very good shape and the consciousness was also not in good shape; the mind was disoriented. It had lost all sense of time and all kinds of Earthly realities. It was in a delirium when that exchange occurred. This was another aspect of the Shelly soul, but what occurs with one aspect affects the other aspects.

The above is from two different readings for Shelly. I was assuming that this was just one soul exchange experience but it would appear that Athor is discussing two different soul exchanges. In each case the inhabiting soul was in deep distress and wished to leave the body. It would seem that other aspects of Shelly's soul had perhaps had a number of soul exchange experiences.

What is the soul's intent in expanding its experience beyond its own system?

If you would wish to have a spiritual explanation it is simply that all are moving or evolving towards the Source (All That Is) but in the process all are experiencing the Source by experiencing itself through billions and billions of manners of ways. This particular soul light has a unique capacity of contracting and expanding simultaneously.

What is the intent of this soul in incarnating at this particular time of the Earth's evolution.

Your particular soul's intent in coming forth in embodiment at this time is in large part due to the fact that you have already experienced not once but three times a so-called dimensional shift. This will actually be the fourth. And so it has come forth, having had this prior experience, with a great deal of knowledge and is here to help others adequately prepare for a similar experience.

Is this soul part of a group soul?

Yes.

Does this soul have other incarnations and existences simultaneous with this one?

In the case of this soul, yes. The others are in other galactic systems or dimensions.

Shelly has had what seems to be contacts from space ships frequently. Can you give some information on that?

It would appear that the Pleiadian system has had much contact with this being as it has spent much time in that system. There are some from the Orion grouping There is a being called Balthazar, a being with great authority and a great commanding presence. He is kind of the main energy that overshadows the transmissions. He is not from the Pleiadian system but is working in conjunction with them somehow. It appears that there are many systems that are working conjointly with you at this time and their species have different appearances, but he is the main one.

We next begin going into lives here on Earth. As usual Athor ends with various visualization and instructions for her continued soul growth which are meant just for Shelley.

Chapter 19
Other Soul Aspects, Parallel Universes, the "Perfect" Soul

From the first time I met Lee I felt she was a very advanced soul. Not only is she a beautiful woman but there was a particular essence which gave her a different quality than most human beings. Although Lee had requested a reading from the Source, this is quite technical and different from most source readings.

We have here a scene of what appears to be almost an egg of light. It is egg shaped, golden colored, somewhat hard substance that has two, rounded parts. It is seen that a ray of light comes like a lightning bolt but it has different colors. It is almost like a violet bluish light that comes and severs the two in half. We are observing a scene wherein a being has put this light on this figure of these two egg like ovoid shapes and has separated the two. This figure is doing a genetic part of manipulations and changes. This being is not satisfied with something regarding this division. It seems that originally the two are identical. When the cells begin to divide, it continues the division process This was produced by the scientific type being and it seems that one of these shapes that has divided has either a different type of energy or more of a certain type of energy than the other. The being doing this experiment thought that there would be equality in the energy of the two halves and it is seen that the being found there was not. This is not your usual soul pattern. What is coming to me is more in questions and words along with the pictures. We still do not know who this being is, but it has on his mind to rectify the experiment. It is an egg energy but nothing like seen on this earth. He leaves the one in this sort of container and he takes the other one into another place and bombards it with a certain type of radiation. In looking at the size of these energy eggs, they are a good handful. Each one is as large as a human hand. In bombarding this other half, there are noises and high frequency noise that come forth from this egg.

There is this tunnel light almost like an interdimensional doorway. There is this tunnel light image which is to represent something similar to this interdimensional warp speed thing. Now it is going through the tunnel and coming out on the other end and the wave and particles of energy go all over the place like this mushroom effect at the bombing of Hiroshima. Now it is coming back in the tunnel. You have been the product of much experimentation. You have also been one who experimented, who did research in different life forms and different dimensional shapes, etc. What we are presently viewing is very difficult to describe. It is part of your energy make up but since this is not earth bound, there is a great difficulty in finding sufficient reference points to adequately explain this.

At the moment, you feel there is a vast expanse in your auric field. The molecular arrangement of your particular field at this time is very loose. There is much space between the different molecules and the molecular bonding is not as tight. This is perhaps just a symbolic representation. We are not certain of the biological reality of this, but let us say we have a picture that the so-called human bonding of the molecular aggregate is one. You have these various chains of molecular bonds. In your case, the bonding is not of this nature at all. Each molecule is seen floating in the field of energy more or less independent of the other in the sense that there is not this aggregate bonding yet there is communication because of the field of energy which exists in which these molecules interact.

The cells in any human being have a telepathic capacity and telepathic resonance and each cell has an intelligence so that is not unique in saying that about yours. We are not saying that you take on everything like a sponge. This is not quite what we would imply here. Because you have been a result of many experiments, your soul has participated in many, many different life cycles of Earth. It has participated in many different types of species and interspecies evolvement. And it has also been several beings in different systems who experimented on other life forms and checked out different things.

There continues to be much discussion about Lee's energy field. Finally Athor sees another scene:

We have here a scene where there is a praying mantis type being. There are yet today beings, so-called extraterrestrial, who are more of an insect type of appearance. You have been one of those in the past. These beings were very interested in genetic mutations, and they had the skill and ability. They were not concerned with Earth, and so your cycle at that time had not been really to do with Earth but there is such a vast background of this type of genetic experimentation and interdimensional experimentation of various energy fields that it would be seen that it would be to your benefit to become aware of this. Yet there is a strong energy against this. One of the beings that is yet connected and working at this time is that race of insect like beings. Because you have done experimentation with some mutations of life form, each one of them is now connected with you and in a sense in you. So that is part of the difficulty of hitting central core. You are a composite of so many different life form energies in the auric field in the psyche, it is quite unique. There are just so many pieces within you.

You have a core identity but it is difficult to grasp because it is so different from most beings that come into human bodies. They do not have this vast long term experience in so many different realities and having done genetic work almost each time. What we are seeing is that you will begin to become much more conscious of this. You will develop a telepathic rapport and connection with some of the main beings that you have had connection with in past existences. There is the praying mantis energy and all of the other extraterrestrial energy because these are all you. It would seem that in your experiments it is almost like your soul wished to find the perfect specimen. We are not getting what that would entail for this quote perfect specimen because it is taking from all these levels and all these existences and its kind for eons. Your soul has stored all of these energies and until finally the soul being is complete. At the moment the soul's experiment is not complete so you are yet searching because all the data and all the energy is not in yet. There is not a vivification of the encodement because the fact that your molecular arrangement is so strewn out in the field it indicates that the encodement has not be vivified.

The aspect of this soul which is a very ancient, very good part of this soul has had umpteen Earth cycles in and of itself. Because of parallel universes, you can go on and on with various descriptions and explanations because of the interrelation of all of these energies on a soul level with this particular soul and its various aspects; it is though this soul and its various aspects has also experienced the same things. Because every aspect of that soul would have equal access to what the other aspect had experienced, depending on the overall picture of what the soul wishes to accomplish. So in other words, each aspect would be programmed (not exact word but the closest we can come) to go off in terms of memory, in terms of recognizing and understanding what some of the other aspects experience at various times. It would be a scene that would be different for every aspect depending again on the soul's general purpose. And this particular soul was able to tap into the memories at this particular time because that is how it had been programmed. But the other aspects of this soul would not necessarily at that precise moment have the full recall of all the other experiences. This is a very difficult concept.

Athor then goes into a series of exercises and visualizations which will assist Lee in recalling these memories.

This is a totally unique experiment. Since it is an experiment there is no one that gives you X amount of words and say this, and this, and this is who you are or that is what you are. It is an ongoing process at this time. It is for your consciousness to develop as a result of this fusion of these different energies from other existences, other frequencies, other dimensions. The consciousness within you must develop. No one can give this to you. It is in the development state. Your soul purpose is to produce that perfect specimen. By perfect we are speaking of a certain energy level. This is not so much to do with any physiological or psychic expression . At this time you have come to this human body to try to complete this through the human vehicle. No one can tell you who or what you will be as a result of the completion of the experiment. This is not said to frighten you because this is not negative. It is simply because it is true. This is part of your prophecy, part of your development. It is your experience and it is your experiment.

At the conclusion of this reading Athor asked if she could scan Lee's body. Athor did not see auras but felt the energy of auric bodies. Since Athor herself was an experiment, she had a scientific interest in beings such as Lee who has such an unusual auric energy.

Chapter 20
An ET Conducting Research in the Ukraine

Matthew is a physics professor at a university. He requested an Athor reading because he has such an intense fascination with Russia. The first question asked if he had any previous lives in Russia.

I have an image of a large hairy boned man working in a snow storm. He is dressed in a heavy coat type thing that seems to be made of furs. He is trying to move against a strong wind and snow pelting down. He is trying to get to this cabin or house which is his destination. The feeling is one of desolation. The being that we are viewing is not desolate, but the surroundings are and the circumstances are desolate. He appears to have come some distance. It was a very harsh journey under extreme weather conditions. And yet there seems to be some urgency in the being traveling like this in this inclement weather. It appears that he is going to a house where his old mother is. The woman is very sick and it is not certain how the message was conveyed but he is going there. He finally reaches the house. The woman is a stout woman, but she is very frail in health at this point. She appears to be in her mid-eighties. She wants to tell him certain things and get certain things straightened out before she passes on as she feels she will die soon. We see that this man is tending to her and is trying to give her some hot soup when she dies in his arms. The man we are viewing in this scene appears to be this being. There is a sadness since the woman meant a great deal to him. The man we are viewing appears to be this being. Again there is a sadness since the woman meant a great deal to him but there is also a strength and a certain detachment. We can't get over the fact of how unusual this energy pattern is because it is not human. He does not have the cloying qualities of certain human emotions. It does not have that heaviness. The being seems to never have sufficiently humanized in a certain way. It seems to be one of the soul's lessons that it wishes to obtain a certain quality through the human realm that it did not have before and it has to do with certain sentiments, certain emotions.

What about Russia? This apparently took place in what was then Russia. I am not sure that explains his emotion.

This is really unusual. We see a space ship. These ships have deposited several beings it is seen. There are approximately nine individuals that were deposited in this area that we are viewing which is part of the Ukraine. There nine spread out within a limited territory. It is seen that there were many other ships that simultaneously did this in other areas of the world as well. Now we are going to focus on these particular ones. These beings are studying the terrain. They are taking samples of vegetation. It is seen that one of the beings wanders into an area where there are animals. This being had never seen an Earth animal before. This is a large type animal on a country/farm area. There are some type of cows and the being continues on over the terrain and sees some goats and chickens. He wishes to take samples but the animals, of course, run away. And so the being does not quite know what to do because these are not stationary objects like the plants. And so the being proceeds on and comes to a farm house. There is a woman, the wife or mother. The other beings seem to be further out in the fields. The being comes into the farm house and the woman faints. He picks her up and puts her on a couch. He is just fascinated because he had not encountered a human being before. He is just looking at her. This being has a humanoid form, but it does not have human type features. The being has long fingers and not five as humans do. He is looking at her, touching the skin and

112

looking at the hands and the head. The woman wakes up and again faints but this is too much for her. The being is just so fascinated and he does not seem to understand her fear. He decides to carry her with him to the ship. There is a discussion on the ship because whatever the problem is at that time, they do not wish to take a human on board. They did not come to Earth for that reason. They came equipped to study other life forms and so he is forced to leave the woman behind. In his way he is very sad because there is a strange longing. He looks around the area and looks at the terrain and looks at the house, and then when he is aboard the ship and it is leaving, he looks at the overall area. There is a longing, a link was made with that being in the place and there may have been other earth lives that bring out more of the particular fascination, but this seems to be the root link.

I give Athor the name of the woman in Russia that Matthew is considering marrying. He has had considerable correspondence with this woman and feels a strong attraction to her.

She was the older woman who was dying and there have been other connections as well.

Was this space ship his first contact with Earth?

Yes.

Matthew: When you are speaking of Russia I almost go unconscious sometimes. I get foreboding feelings about learning the language or that I must just start speaking it.

Matthew is thinking of actually moving to Russia.

The only thing I am getting is that there was some kind of revolution in the Czar's time.

Matthew: My great grandfather fought in Russia.

This is really confusing to me. (comment by Evelyn).

Matthew: Not to me. It is amazing to me how you mirror my internal discussions at this point about the ship.

113

Sometimes it seems that one part of me is just human, no different than anyone else yet there is one part me that never seems to have the connections that I think I should have. It is clear to me that psychologically compared to most I am pretty strong.

Matthew: I can't remember anything when I am four to five years old. Why is that?

All I can get is that your essence has been a willing participant in several experiments of interspecies cross cultural interspecies bondings. And this is on other levels which in your essential state you comprehend. However, the human brain as yet cannot interpret these experiences with any logical degree of accuracy. Any lack of memory is a direct result of some of these experiments.

As the reading was ending, Athor once again asked for the name of the client.

Your name does not fit. It just doesn't fit your energy at all.

Athor once again asked if she could feel his aura to try and get more information. Many of my clients felt a strong extraterrestrial connection, but Matthew's feeling was particularly strong. One of his questions was to ask who his real mother is since he feels very little connection with his Earth mother. This question per se was not really answered but it would be surmised from everything that Matthew told me that his real parents were extraterrestrials as was the case with Athor. Matthew seemed perfectly comfortable with his ET roots. This was a particularly interesting case that I clearly remember many years after the reading. I feel that it was an honor to have this fascinating soul request an Athor reading!

Chapter 21
A Genetically Engineered Drone

We would like to begin with the Source of this soul.

This soul energy resonates with what you would term a very narrow band frequency as it is indicated here that the name resonates to a narrow band of light that we are following. We have here an image of an explosion. It would almost appear to be a planetary type of explosion or something of a similar magnitude. It is uncertain as yet whether this is a physical plane dimension or not. There is much smoke and turbulence, much vibrational activity in many different directions and frequencies. This being it appears was what you would term violently ejected from the plane upon which it spent considerable time. This is almost akin to an astral explosion. It does not appear to be physical, however, neither is of the finer densities for these things do not occur on the frequencies of light. Please proceed with your questions.

One of Anna's primary concerns is lingering depression. She would like to know the root cause of her depression.

It appears that this being eons ago was what you might term a drone worker in a certain planetary sphere which is not in your present galactic system. This type of worker excavated mineral ores and things of this nature. The term drone does not imply one without mentality but one who was bred for a specific purpose. This was at a time when there were all types of genetic engineering going on in this certain planetary sphere. These things are just beginning upon the planet earth. They have existed elsewhere for eons of time. There appears to be some type of accident. It was not created by the beings who were excavating on the planet but rather an occurrence which occurred due to certain combinations of gaseous mixtures which came from the interstellar space through what would appear to be some type of vehicle that came over the surface of the area where these people were working and excavating. The gases which were emitted from this vehicle were of an extremely destructive nature. The beings in the immediate vicinity for approximately a distance of two hundred and fifty miles from the focal point were catapulted up above the surface of the planet. It was not what you would term a physical explosion. It was as though these gases, these energy frequencies drew out the full soul essence. It drew out the astral bodies; it drew out all the other layers and levels from within the physical vehicle that were then excavating on this planet. And this was what exploded outward as indeed these physical types were in essence destroyed. Here we have this tremendous explosion of all these other bodies and beings going outward into space as it were.

Now it is seen that the being was in a state of not only utter confusion but of great sadness which makes for a certain type of unknowing and not knowing exactly what the feelings were. The beings which were genetically engineered for this particular project were of such a nature that they were not equipped with the consciousness to develop an awareness of their higher natures; the method of engineering was such as to effectively block the higher centers and to disallow the development of a full being in the truest spiritual sense. It is noted that the being then went into what you would term a state of hibernation, a state like being in a gray void of great energy swirling about and a nothingness existing. The being was only aware of this gray swirling mass of energy which had no particular focus point nor did it have a beginning and an end. The being was simply in that energy and could not dis-identify with that energy as the centers were not operational due to the engineering which had been done unfortunately. So this is the root cause of the depression.

It is seen that at this time in this life cycle the being has undertaken a most courageous proposition. It has undertaken to vivify the centers which were so lacking in life force or life energy as it were and wishes to go beyond and overcome these energies, frequencies and memories. It is seen that this being has a particularly strong vibratory frequency deep within the heart chakra. This being has much capacity of a soft, giving nature. The being has much emotional depth which is yet often hidden deep within the heart. It is seen that as this being develops and utilizes this loving capacity and focuses primarily on the heart chakra utilizing various techniques *(which Athor goes into later)* then the higher centers will open and with that opening dissipate these memories and these energies and these nebulous of clouds on nothingness which are indeed but a memory.

The rest of the reading is mainly about her relationships with certain people in her life. I was frankly appalled to hear that Anna was a drone. However, she did not appear to be disturbed as I and fortunately Athor went into a really peaceful lifetime following a number of traumatic lifetimes.

We have here a very pleasant lifetime. This is close to your heart. We see a tribe of aborigines and a particular small child who is out in the bush. This appears to be a relatively peaceful, joyful, grass roots type of lifetime wherein the being was allowed to enjoy its environment and to enjoy itself. It was not ruled nor was it put in any position where it had to do any particular thing. It was simply allowed to be and to exercise itself in any way that it chose to. Thus you have a strong love in your heart for the Australian continent for you are very well versed in the land formations and topography of that nation. Through the joy of sharing and coming to know the land, the creatures, the plants and the trees, the being began to achieve a spiritual understanding. These aborigines have their extrasensory apparatus functioning in the areas where the so-called civilized white man does not. They are tuned into a frequency of hearing which is not typical of the western civilized people. Their hearing capacity is extremely acute and thus they are able to hear not only sounds from this realm but the astral sounds as well. Thus they are in close communication with certain parts of the spirit realm. This sensory apparatus was functioning in the Lemurian people though it was not in such evidence upon the Atlantian continent and its people.

The reading ends with more suggestions to overcome the trauma of being a drone and the subsequent explosion. Athor told Anna that she has a beautiful soul light and to call upon the forces of God to assist her in releasing these traumatic memories.

Chapter 22
A Transitional Energy

Kate has felt fear throughout her life and also an intensely violent energy like ripping the fabric of time and space. She wonders why she is so afraid.

We have here an explosion. It is not on this planet. It has the appearance of an atomic blast. This was an experiment on another planet. We have the image of a being in the nucleus of this explosion. The being is held there, it is somewhat akin to being in the eye of a hurricane. There are all these types of gamma rays going towards this being, coming out of the being, there is tremendous force. The being has a form although it is semi-solid, not entirely etheric nor is it solidly physical. The being had volunteered for this experiment. This was something that had not been done before and it was something obviously that they knew very little about as to the end result. It is seen that at the culmination of this experience there were certain things that came out of the form of that being. We are not saying that they were entities but they were like semi-solid masses of energies and each one of these semi-solid masses of energies began an independent life form. It was an entirely different creation that the being was made of at that time. It was like in another dimensional reality another substance was added as a result of this experiment. Essentially many different life forms were created. However, it is seen that these forms were what we would term "soul-less". They were the creation of an experimental nature and this was more scientific rather than creative. The beings were more like androids but were not of that type of substance. The substance of the beings was such that it was extremely malleable, something in Earth terms like 'silly putty'.

Now we are going into the fear. It is seen that the being that emerged from that experience was somewhat altered, not completely because the being in a sense remained intact. It was basically bombarded with all these rather new energies and as a result these new beings were created.

Something seems to be blocking the information about the cause of Anna's fear. Go to another question and we will see where that goes.

Anna asks, "Did I walk into this existence in my young childhood years?"

We see that this was a transitional experiment. We do not have accurate terminology because we do not see this quite as a soul exchange of the type that we are commonly referring to. The term "transitional changes" comes to mind and this dealt with not only an altered state but another energy. It was not another being, per se, but it is almost like a time warp factor and it is not accurate to say that it is a future self. There were energies from other dimensional realms, there was an essence from other dimensions. All these energies from many different dimensions were brought together, which unified the essence of this being. What was the name at birth? (*Anna had changed her name*).

Her original name was given.

From the vibratory frequency we get an entirely different energy only in the sense that it was much more grounded than you are. This is not to say that you are a flake, but this energy that you spoke of was much more solidified. It was an energy that could have led a very contented existence in the material world. It would have led a very good Earth life but without having any openings to speak of into any other realms and realities. This transitional energy entered when you were two and a half years old.

Anna: I awoke on 6/12/97 in the middle of the night to remember condensing down from an expanded state and floating into my bedroom as a young child. The experience felt so confining and contracted. I then felt a 'veil' of forgetfulness come over me and I was left with sadness. I also felt immediate fear which has continued to the present time. What is the meaning of the intense, paralyzing energy bursts, white light and great energy that I've experienced throughout the years? It was always followed with rejuvenation and joy the following day, and I felt the presence of kind loving beings nearby".

That is simply a continuation of the experiment so to speak. These beings that are here today are obviously part of this whole procedure and they are extremely loving beings. They touch this one's heart in a certain frequency of recognition. They are interested in infusing certain combination of frequencies into the mass density of a physical vehicle. This is not new for you as a being because obviously you have done similar things as described from that former experiment. This is basically a continuation of your essence and its purpose. It is seen that your essence in the overall span of this existence has had many, many experiences offering itself for experimental purposes to further the cosmic evolutionary procedure. This is basically just a continuation. These beings are able to transmit tonal frequencies that can be perceived but it is difficult for this being to allow them to transmit these tonal frequencies which are their most expedient mode of communication because the wiring of the brain patterning is not entirely receptive to the translation of these tonal patternings.

Anna: With the aid of a shaman I recently uncovered vivid memories of being forcibly held down in a non-ordinary reality, and some type of beings drawing the life energy out of me. I was struggling and angry but could not stop them. I felt young. My friend said they damaged the cord to my eighth chakra and he worked on re-connecting it. Who were these beings and what was happening?"

Some beings came into this room with you. It must be these beings because just before you started asking that question a cap came over my head trying to block the reading. We will try to bull doze through. It is seen that the nature of this being desires to be of service and its former experimental nature has put it into many different dimensional realms. These dimensional realms are not always positive. The being accidentally entered one or several of these realms. This last experience was not in a physical location, this was an in-between like the astral realm of Alpha Centauri. There was an energy belt around that system and these beings came through that energy belt. I cannot say that you will never again encounter these kinds of beings but one of your important lessons is to gain navigational awareness. You need to develop an ability to traverse these realms without being caught in this manner. You are in a sense a cosmic shaman. You travel in cosmic realms and you do very similar things on these other levels although maybe not consciously yet but very similar things that the Earth based shamans do in the Earthly realm.

Anna: "I have the feeling that two opposing groups of beings are performing some kind of experiment as to whether Light will win out. There seems to be a group who are intent on harming me, yet another group teaching me wonderful ways to experience and express the Light."

It is not that this being is marked, it is the Process. This being has undertaken a rather unique and extremely important undertaking. In a sense what this being is doing or attempting to do through the physical is creating roadways, opening up energetic pathways. It is a pioneer. It is charting new territory. It would be akin to your pioneers who came to America and settled the West. They went through treacherous mountain passes and horrendous weather. Many died and so on. Well, here we have a being who has undertaken this pioneering journey to break open this new frontier and make these energetic openings so that others can do their thing so to speak. This is a very vital process. She is charting on a cosmic scale similar to what the Earth shamans are doing primarily through the Earth sphere.

The higher frequencies of your soul essence purpose is to recognize that you have 15 to 20 beings assisting you in this work. Part of your lesson is to not allow the sense of alone-ness to cut off any further training or progress in these realms. Whatever techniques you can find that will help you bridge the gap or will help you deal with that fear and that alone-ness would be wise to go into because your experiment itself is very important.

Next Athor gives suggestions on various techniques to overcome the fear and feelings of being alone. I finally ask for more clarification on this transitional energy.

As I understand it this experiment took place when Anna was two and a half. The old soul is still here. Is that correct?

The so-called "old soul" is also in a transitional space.

Please explain.

The original soul and this other transitional soul are both growing together.

Anna: Do I have group of people from other realms?

Yes, they are identifying themselves as Nilisks. They are from a star system in the seven sisters, the Pleiades. There are approximately 1500 different species in that system so this is simply just one group.

Anna: I have always wondered if I have a cosmic name.

What comes in is ELANA. We suggest that you take each tone of this name and sound it. Like "E"... and do this daily. You will find some remarkable things happening. It will more fully anchor more of your essence.

Anna is a very beautiful soul. She embodies the very essence of the real Christ spirit. She has become a good friend and I totally admire her as an extremely spiritual person although she understandably feels very different from the people around her which creates a feeling of loneliness. As you can tell it seemed best to simply let her ask many of her own questions since she was there in person for the reading.

Chapter 23
Another Existence in the Angelic Realm

We would like to begin by tracing the soul roots from the Source.

We have here a form that has some very defined shape which is very similar to a humanoid form. However, this form does not have what is termed a sensor type consciousness at this time that we are viewing. It has a most rudimentary form of consciousness and it is not physical in form. It is as though the being took on this form in order to experience the sensation of this particular sphere although the sensory apparatus was not very like that which is on the Earth and through the physical bodies. It was almost as though the being is an intermediate step from a seemingly totally formless almost void to the beginning rudimentary stages of form.

It is seen that in that form the being had the capacity to be most flexible; it was almost like your mercury; it could take different shapes and then it would spring back to its original form per se. But it could also become quite amorphous. The form has taken on an amorphous quality and the being seems to be just spreading out over this particular area, flattening out and in a sense merging in a rather amorphous manner. You couldn't call it a form, but there was some substance to it. There was more to it than just simple energy.

What dimension was this and was this in this galaxy?

We hear it is the eighth, but it is not of this system so it does not follow in your evolutionary linage.

We now have a form that seems to be quite a leap. Perhaps there was some in between but this is the next we are seeing. It appears to be an angelic type of being. This is not as dense as the other existence which we viewed. It is much

125

lighter, but it has substance, it has form again. It almost appears to have the quality of your protective angels, the ones in particular who deal with the healing faculties and healing qualities. It was different from the human sense in that the love nature is very, very different. There is less of a density in the love nature and in other faculties as well. The being is one with the forces and the energies of that particular plane at that time. It simply wished to experience that particular density and that particular form.

This being was more ethereal than most. It just simply wished to experience that form of evolution. We will leave it at that. We do not see any particular duties or responsibilities that it assumed because it appears that this being has taken on many different shapes and many forms in past cycles for the simple experiencing of these rather than perhaps any particular defined and focused mission. The desire was perhaps more one of experiencing these different levels simply for the experiencing of it.

It is seen that in the angelic form the being had communication with beings which appear to be very similar to the earth plane beings; it is seen that the beings seem to hover in that strata where there were denser beings nearby you might say. We see one particular small child here that it has kind of hovered over in that state. It was almost like an exchange occurred there. It was like the being was studying this species and this particular child and it was giving of its nature and of itself in the energy frequencies to that being while at the same time going from that denser being and gathering information and learning. So there was quite an equitable exchange at that time.

It is seen as a result of this study, the being acquired an interest you might say into coming into this type of evolutionary strain. That is where the beginning desire arose from that point to go into a denser form and experience other dimensions and denser realities. This being has a unique capacity because of its background and because of its evolutionary experiences. There have been other cycles in between. It is seen that it stayed in the angelic realm for quite some time. In that process it evolved from the point of just simply wishing to experience the energies and so forth which was a much less personalized thing to a more individualized essence. It acquired a rudimentary sense of personality though the angelic realms are different in that sense but none the less there was a similarity as the individuality increased. As the consciousness of this being increased the desire to experience the human plane increased.

It was not quite certain yet how to affect this rather quantum leap in evolution in terms of exchanging one form for another which were seemingly light years apart. The being belonged to a legion of angelic beings that had a certain function. They were almost like the guardians but something very similar, the watchers. And these beings would frequent not exactly the lower astral realms, but they would frequent the astral realms immediately penetrating the Earth plane and they would spend considerable amounts of time there in trying to be of assistance in the energetic affairs and fluxes of this planet and the beings and creatures upon it. This being graduated shall we say to that status and so it took a long time coming down and through this astral plane.

Now there was a very sudden loss of consciousness it would seem because when it entered a certain vibratory frequency of the astral plane it was as though a vortex of energy sucked it down. As long as it remained beyond that level that did not occur but here at this point the loss of consciousness occurred which had been very slowly built up in a step-by-step process in this being's evolution in building up the awareness and the consciousness. It did not go into great quantum shifts. There was a sensation of this great downward spiral and this downward pull and the consciousness was transferred into what appears to be an Earth vehicle. We do not see the birth process but we do see a young boy who appears to be at a very primitive time in the Earth's evolution in terms of when the woods were pristine and nature was at its height. It was not at the time of what you would term the caveman or the dinosaurs. It appears to be at a much nicer time wherein the elements were all working harmoniously together and it was almost as though there was a so-called Garden of Eden. The being subsisted on plant life, fruits and things of that sort. We do not see that there was any killing involved at that time as it appears to have been primarily vegetarian. We see a small clan, family unit. They have dwellings made out of reeds and grasses and things of this sort, a few sticks or logs here and there to hold up the structure, but primarily things were woven and put together from vegetation.

Marie has a long list of questions so may we more on? Apparently Marie has been visited by extraterrestrials. Through regressions with me, we were able to get quite a bit of information regarding her abductions. Can you get more details?

This goes back to one of these early Earth lives wherein it is seen that a connection was made with this being at that time. It is seen that the purity and innocence of this being at that time was a most attractive vibratory frequency to those from other realms who were indeed already upon the Earth and visiting the Earth. This has been an ongoing process for eons of time; it is seen that this connection was made during that very first cycle. It is like an agreement has been made on some level between the soul of this being and the various beings with which it has communicated on Earth or had contact. This is different from those who have been implanted. This being has a certain lack of density on certain levels which permits access to certain energy frequencies and combinations and communication which is not as easily affected with others except through implant devices. Because of her energy field this being has a basic opening and has agreed to allow this influx to occur of exchanging of energies in a certain sense. The soul has made an agreement for furthering its own experience, to allow these connections to occur.

Can you tell us where these extraterrestrial beings are from?

There have been different ones. There are many beings from many systems which can gather much information and learning through tapping on these certain frequencies through Earth beings. This is much easier with Marie because of her unique frequency arrangement. This is not seen by the soul as an invasion of any type but rather this is a continuation of agreements that are being carried out for the mutual benefit for all concerned. Are you aware of the shape of the beings who have contacted you in this lifetime?

Marie: Yes, I am but I really try not to think about it.

We see a fairly dense form. These do not appear to be very tall. They do not appear to have any negative properties. They are simply alien if you will. They have rudimentary humanoid characteristics. They are very similar in shape but there are many differences. They do not have as many fingers on the hand; the orifices of the ears are different in size and the eyes are much larger. These beings we are seeing seem to be linked to the Orion system.

What is Marie's connection to Metatron?

This is a very powerful frequency. He is coordinating various activities of various fleets. They all have slightly different functions. Some are sent to study certain samples upon the planet. Some are sent to make contact with certain beings. Because of past cycles with this unique frequency range there have been repeated contacts in the past. There has been a soul agreement made on your part to both assist and be of assistance to these beings and others who would wish to help in the evolvement of the species upon this planet and would wish to help in the changes which are about to occur because for you it has always been a matter of interest for the experience.

Marie is a beautiful young woman who came from a rather well to do family. Looking at her one would think she had few problems in this Earth life, but she has suffered from bouts of depression and has learning disabilities. The rest of the reading was devoted to methods of dealing with these problems as well as giving her insights into her soul connection with a number of individuals. She has an aura about her that seems to attract people. I have no doubt that she will be one of those Light workers who is helping the planet evolve.

Chapter 24
Higher Self Experiment and another
Relationship with Metatron

This is a remote reading. Thomas asked for a reading from the source, but he has also had what he feels is a walk-in experience and would like clarification of this.

What we are viewing here is a peculiar arrangement of energies. It almost looks as though parts of the old being were released. We do not see a clear-cut exchange at that time *(he had given a date in 1975)*. It is more that there were parts of the old being that were released. There was a tremendous inner auric turmoil we see on a very deep inner level. The entire auric field was in an uproar and the elements of the old psyche were released. This is an unusual configuration because this is not commonly what occurs in an incarnation process that this much of the old psyche was purged. There was some other date. It is seen that the full process of the exchange occurred at that date. There was rather more a purging and a cleansing and it is seen that in actuality it is more of the higher essence of the being that was then able to establish a greater resonance through the vehicle. We will go into the soul's origins and see what occurs.

We have here a light and an explosion. The next image that comes is like two curved rays of light that come together almost as though in a 'V' shape that suddenly seems to become many as they are spiraling. They become like a gyroscope with many strands of light spiraling within it and around it and through it. The gyroscopic configuration of many light rays seems to be a consciousness. It is just oscillating at this moment. Then there is another explosion within this gyroscopic light field. We see a light that is ejected from the center of this. And this light goes out into the universe. It is a rather large light. The light again splits and it is seen that there are several locations in the universe seeded with the energy from that light. It is seen that from each of these seed pods, in a sense of light, beings were eventually formed, colonizing on various systems. We have not encountered this type of formation before. They were all of the same consciousness of the same grouping, but they were almost like they were cloned. They had variations but it was like they were all controlled by the same consciousness yet they had various distinct differences within each individual being. Okay, the date that this being gave what occurred was that all these various facets from this central consciousness went back so to speak. They left his being in the physical. In a sense it was like another rebirth as we are looking at this gyroscope of strands of light. This is a similar occurrence here although we do not see the gyroscopic form. There was an explosion within that being of a similar birthing process. What has occurred is not a walk-in experience. This is very different.

We are still looking at these various systems and the various beings that colonized them. The central intelligence or consciousness never materialized except in the various parts. So there was this central consciousness and the central intelligence which then split. So the central intelligence of consciousness was in a strange way apart from all these clone appearing beings. We only use the word clone because there were great similarities between all of them and they all belonged to that central form of intelligence that chooses to manifest through these types of forms. These forms were numerous and on many systems. Each was adhering to that central intelligence, each being guided by this central intelligence from which they all sprang. In a smaller sense this can be likened to the principle of The All That Is manifesting in various and in sundry forms throughout many universes. This is just on a smaller scale.

Is there any one particular soul that was in the body of Thomas?

There is a soul light, but we would hesitate to call it a soul in your terminology because it is simply an extension of this greater unit. The being is very well aware of this consciousness, of this greater reality. There is great difficulty with bringing in these units of energy of light into a physical plane dimension and expecting the unit to function in a coherent manner. It is seen that there is great difficulty between the various factions within that being, and so many just left. It would be incorrect to say they were individual souls because they were just simply reflections of the great whole. They were not individualized as soul entities. This does not make them less.

What was left after these lights left?

We see one light. It is part of the grouping. They cannot be individualized as being something separate. When you are dealing with a human consciousness, the human consciousness wishes to identify. It wishes to bring into smaller and smaller units so that it can hopefully comprehend what is almost impossible at the time to comprehend with the limited consciousness. It is not comprehensible to the logical pathways so it requires the opening of the greater consciousness, what you would term your intuitive side and beyond. Words are very difficult to describe this particular existence of this energy. Thomas is having equal difficulty at times in determining who he is. In trying to function through the human consciousness this energy does not have the capacity and does not have the restrictions. And so to filter this type of concept through the human mind and through its physical form functioning with a human brain, it makes it rather difficult. There is nothing you can relate to on the human plane to try and pigeon hole this consciousness. This body of the Thomas being is simply a vehicle for this consciousness to expand itself and try to remember itself. It is a rather odd terminology considering the vastness of this consciousness. It is almost as though the consciousness as a whole is seeking to define itself. Though the body itself has the capacity to be very structured and very organized and very rigid in a sense, the energy itself being so unbounded, limitless, there is a great tug of war in a sense within the auric field since this experiment occurred. It is like the energy is still trying to adjust and to adapt. There are many restrictions of the human realm that this energy is not familiar with. There is a constant juggling on a certain level within this being where there is a continual equalization occurring for the being to be able to function and to come to terms with this essence.

Can you go into some of the existences after this soul went to different planets?

There is a being who appears to be almost like an engineer of some type. The being is calculating, doing figures and things of this sort. It is like a mining operation. I see machinery that is very similar to Earth but the atmosphere does not have a sun. They are trying to get into a mountainside. There is a gateway within this mountain that has been covered. This machinery is digging away at the covering to the entrance. The entrance leads them into an underground world. This group of beings goes down and they enter; there are rivers and streams and water type bodies of water. They come into this valley with something like a blue sun although it is not a sun. The light seems to stream all over. We cannot see the source of it. This is an isolated and protected valley in the center of this region. They set up some type of devices there because they wished to harness this light energy or wished to study it. The energy from this light in this valley is deflected off of their instruments which does not cause them undue surprise. As it is deflected, it begins to concentrate. It concentrates into a ball of energy, a rather large but very dense ball of energy. Before it was just a light and defused through the whole atmosphere in that valley, the instrumentation that these beings used concentrated it into a dense form of energy which has a very strong intelligence. The being at that time wished to solidify and wished to identify itself. The being has had a long standing history of wishing to identify itself. By being able to isolate or in a sense bring together the varying parts of that energy, he hoped at that point in that existence to identify it. He began communicating with it. As he stood there in this valley, this bluish ball of energy and he had an energy exchange that was very dramatic and important. Because parts of the energy of this ball of blue went into that being's system at that time and parts were released from his system into the ball. That was his means and manner of communication. He collects energy from his experiences.

It is seen that this particular being has had several encounters with this energy in varying forms and existences. It always sought to communicate and manifest a greater portion of it in whatever realm that particular being was in at the time.

Let me see if I understand what you are saying. At birth this being was a collection of energy and when he had this so called walk-in experience (sudden change in consciousness) that was when part of his group was released. Is this correct?

Yes, but it is not correct to call it even a group. We are having difficulty finding the right word to adequately express this. Yes, they were just different aspects of this energy that were released which then opened the way for a certain frequency of what your humans would term the higher mind of a particular essence to come through. The energy basically just surrounds the being and it is throughout the entire auric field. It can only be called an overshadowing presence by someone who would look at it superficially because of the manner in which it shows on the energy field. If you look deeper you can see that it is a reflection of that main intelligence. To try to establish a concrete identifying pattern to this type of intelligence is not easy because it is so vast and so broad.

I ask what Thomas can do to help him in understanding who he really is.

Athor gives a long exercise which Thomas later called the North Star meditation. Athor is referring to Polaris.

Thomas later requested a follow-up reading. He states that when he did the North Star meditation something definitely happened. Can you tell Thomas what happened?

It is seen that what might be considered bi-polar energies from one of the inner dimensional planes of the North Star have interfaced with both the etheric astral and mental vehicles of this being, bringing them into closer alignment as it is seen that there was a disturbance between these vehicles though it was not a permanent one. These vehicles would periodically go into disarray and where there would be one that would be out of sync that would affect the others as well. This in itself is not unique or unusual but it is a blessing that the alignment has been accepted. It is seen that along with the alignment there is a connection that has not been made with the main energies of the North Star system. The being's vehicles are preparing for a type of transitional experience.

Thomas wrote that he was having some serious health problems. "I was told that by the end of this year all of my affairs will be in order and the death of the body will occur approximately eight to twelve months hence. Is this correct?"

This is correct only if the being wishes it to be. It is seen that there is the possibility for the so-called freeing of the consciousness within the period of approximately thirteen months from now. However, it is also seen that this could be a time of a different type of transitional stage in which the consciousness enters what might be termed a unique level of awareness and the connection to the physical will be altered in such a way that there will still be a functionality within the physical, but the normal pathways of usual attachments that are seen in the usual vehicles would not be there. So there is a choice. The being may completely disconnect through that physical vehicle in that time period of approximately thirteen months or the being may opt to change the realm of consciousness as had been indicated. This cannot be explained much further because it is an experiential level which will then be undergone at that time. The decision will be made approximately three to four weeks prior to the actual experience as to which way the being will go.

Thomas states that the name of the one that his group sprang forth from is Alteria where units are called Alterians, information given to him at the completion of the North Star meditation. Is this correct?

This is as close an approximation as one needs.

Thomas asks about his main guide, Metatron. What can you tell us about this being?

The energy which has been termed Metatron is first and foremost a multi-dimensional frequency. This multi-dimensional frequency exists simultaneously in many, many realms. It has several so-called identities in these varying realms. For the purposes of those beings who are unable to bring the totality of this consciousness together, so Metatron being a multi-dimensional energetic frequency comes and goes. We see an image of the energy expanding and contracting, expanding and contracting and in each phase of expansion there are events which occur in various dimensions that are attributed to the Metatron energetic frequencies. In the point of contraction there is assimilation of the God force, a concentration. It is very similar to the in breath and out breath of the All That Is. So the Metatron energy is but one representation of that sequence of that consciousness. To state that Metatron is a being is highly incorrect. This is not so. It is not a being in the sense humans understand beings. It has never had a physical expression per se. However, as part of its creative evolutionary aspect, this Metatron energy has taken a great interest in certain of the occurrences of this planetary sphere you call Earth. And thus it has made contact through in a very limited fashion. Again we emphasize, do not bring this consciousness into such a limited box because it is far greater than that.

This concluded the questions asked by Thomas. My, what an unusual soul! Again apparently the Athor material was apparently understood by Thomas, but to me this seemed a great deal like science fiction. Of course, many of these readings seem like science fiction, but this one impressed me as being particularly bizarre. I had very little information about Thomas when we began the first reading, but in the second requested reading he revealed that he had established a spiritual center and was very much into healing. As with many of the people who have undergone these various experiments with energy, his physical body was having great difficulty handling all these unusual energies. The reading ended with Athor giving Thomas some additional exercises to further understand who he really is.

I want to add that in the Jewish religion Metatron is considered an archangel which seems to perhaps be logical under the umbrella of the description by Athor.

Chapter 25
God and Angels

It was a great privilege to have a highly intellectual, spiritual man request numerous Athor readings over a period of years when I was working with Athor. He has enough readings to write his own book about the Athor wisdom. The readings were mainly about his business and personal life, but often he would ask philosophical questions. He wanted a more in-depth definition of God.

God as we understand it is another term for the All That Is. The All That Is is an energy that permeates all life. It imbues and surrounds and interpenetrates all life. By that we are speaking of all the way through the mineral kingdom, the animal, the vegetable, and the human, etc. This is not limited to the physical but goes into many planes and dimensional realities. The All that Is differentiates itself into many various forms, frequencies, some of which are represented in terms of light. Some manifest into some type of physical form, therefore, there is nothing which is not of God.

In this differentiation process there is indeed a higher hierarchical arrangement of sorts. In the particular universe the hierarchical arrangement consists of beings who have achieved varying levels of spiritual evolution, understanding, attunement, etc. In that hierarchical arrangement, the angelic kingdom has chosen to offer its assistance to many and varied life forms, some of which we feel is human. The archangels of this angelic kingdom have a much broader range and purpose of manifesting the God force. Each type of being that has evolved to a certain level thus emits a certain series of frequencies of the God force. In the human realm there are indeed many and varied frequencies which are given forth, which are transmitted of the God force, depending on the consciousness of the individual being. In the angelic realm it is not so differentiated. This thought force and this energy are indeed acting as a transformer. And so the energy from the higher and higher realm in this hierarchy arrangement is then stepped down and the angels themselves play a very significant role in this transforming capacity. Without this kingdom, the human kingdom would be in a sense lost from the God force which is a very strange concept to human beings. The angelic realm in stepping down these energies from the so called higher realm into the human kingdom enables the human consciousness thus to become increasingly more aware of its own needs and its own divinity.

Chapter 26
Concluding Remarks

As the reader will note, many of these soul histories begin with an explosion. We humans think of an explosion as something that is of a destructive nature, but in these readings Athor is really referring to ENERGY. She was very much into feeling and sensing energy while he/she was here in a body on Earth.

What I have always pictured as the birthing of a soul is akin to fireworks. In a sense this is like an explosion with sparks going out from the nucleus. I watch fireworks with a total sense of awe; they are such a beautiful display of God-like energy. While many of these Off-Earth experiments may seem frightening, they are simply various ways that the All That Is expresses itself. My own history of Off-Earth existences described in my book *Cosmic Relationships* is quite bizarre and might be interpreted as disturbing, but since I had no individualized consciousness during the beginning phases of my soul, I have no memory of these existences and viewed them simply as scientific interest. While I was shocked at the information in some of these readings, my clients and those who requested remote readings to my knowledge never registered any trauma as the result of the readings but rather a new understanding of their present lifetimes here on Earth. However, until I had determined that a client was emotionally stable, I did not suggest an Athor reading. Those who received their readings remotely as the result of hearing about Athor in *From Sirius to Earth* were seemingly highly evolved spiritually savvy people who had taken the brave step of requesting a reading.

My goal in writing the Athor Wisdom books is to help the planet evolve by opening the door to other dimensions and assisting people in understanding that the spirit takes on many forms and has many experiences prior to coming to Earth. There is no conflict between evolution and creationism. This is not the straight Darwinian type evolution of one species evolving into another, but each soul inhabiting various forms until it finally makes the decision to incarnate on Earth. Actually the whole soul is too vast to incarnate, so it is only one aspect of the soul that inhabits a body and then leaves the body at death to go again into other realms.

These readings often leave more questions than answers as far as I am concerned, but my goal was to have Athor address as many questions of the clients as possible during the time period allotted for the reading. Athor's energy was depleted after about an hour so this also limited the amount of time devoted to each session. There were many times when I wanted to get more information to explain some of these bizarre Off-Earth existences, but that would have slowed down the session since Athor had no sense of time while in a trance state, and she would go into great detail and I had to move her along to address the next question. I would very much like to hear from people who had Athor readings giving their feedback on how the readings have helped them. While a number of people wrote giving their appreciation of their readings, I did not hear from some of them subsequent to receiving their readings. I know that my Athor readings helped me a great deal in understanding my own soul and the important relationships in my life. The world was quite different in the early 90's and very possibly the readings would be even more relevant in this present day chaotic world.

I am presenting this material as a means to open up the minds of people here on Earth to the fact that many, many people have had extraterrestrial experiences and if

144

extraterrestrials should decide to land here on Earth in a manner that will leave no doubt of their presence, there is no need to panic. You probably noted that many of the beings wish to colonize on various planets and that may include the Earth. These beings could bring much needed technological assistance in cleaning up the pollution of our planet and giving us advanced methods of healing the human body. There are some negative extraterrestrials, but we are being told by the Ascended Masters that the Earth is being cleansed of the negative forces that interfered with our evolution. If one should feel any fear, call on the God Force and surround yourself with White Light.

We are all one in this great cosmic adventure!